A Gift To Myself

A Personal Workbook and Guide To Healing My Child Within

Charles L. Whitfield, M.D.

Health Communications, Inc.
Deerfield Beach, Florida

Charles L. Whitfield
21 West Road
Baltimore, Maryland 21204
(301) 825-0041

Publisher: Health Communications, Inc.
          3201 S.W. 15th Street
          Deerfield Beach, Florida 33442-8124

Cover design by Reta Thomas

Acknowledgments

Special thanks to Bruce Fischer, Herbert L. Gravitz, Mary Jackson, Karen Jones, Rebecca Peres, Donna O'Toole and Ralph Raphael who read an early draft of this book and offered constructive suggestions.

Grateful acknowledgmont is given to the following for permission to reprint: "Who I Really Am" chart on page 20, adapted and modified from Howard Halpern: *How To Break Your Addiction To A Person.* McGraw-Hill, NY, 1982. © Howard Halpern; by permission of McGraw-Hill and the author.

Section by Gay Hendricks from his book *Learning To Love Yourself,* Prentice-Hall, Englewood Cliffs, NJ, 1982. © Gay Hendricks; by permission of Prentice-Hall, Englewood Cliffs, NJ.

Jacket copy reproduced by permission of The Free Press from *SOLITUDE: A Return To The Self* by Anthony Storr; ©1988 by Macmillan, Inc.

American Psychiatric Association's Severity Rating of Psychosocial Stressors from DSM-III, ©1980 American Psychiatric Association.

Timmen Cermak's quotes from his book *Diagnosing And Treating Co-dependence,* ©1986 by The Johnson Institute.

The poem "Please Hear What I'm Not Saying" ©1966 by Charles C. Finn.

> This book is dedicated to Nancy,
> who was awakening to her Child Within.

I would like to acknowledge the following three people for their contributions to this book — Roberta Reinhard of Washington, DC, for desk top publishing, Pat Ross of Carmel, California, for the photo and Suzette Billedeaux of Salt Lake City, Utah, for drawing the *Child in Hiding.*

Contents

Introduction

Neither I nor any other person has the answers for you. I wrote this book to help anyone interested to find their own answers inside them. My sense is that we each have our answers inside. You have your answers for you. I believe that those answers are inside you, as you — as your Child Within.

In this book I describe an approach to recovery and healing that I have seen help people in their process of getting free from the bondage of co-dependence and having grown up in a dysfunctional family.

I suggest that to get the most benefit that you work through this book *slowly*, over the course of from three to five years.

I hope that you will put it down frequently. Allow at least one or two weeks or more between working through each exercise.

When doing an exercise, read through the whole section or chapter once. Then return and read it more slowly. And then *take a lot of time* to work through that exercise.

Should you have any inordinate difficulty with any of this material or questions about it — or if you would like to go deeper and heal your Child Within more completely — you might consider contacting a therapist or counselor with expertise in helping co-dependent people and adult children of dysfunctional families.

While **I am unable to offer consultations by mail or by telephone, or to make referrals to a therapist in your area,** I have suggested some approaches to finding a therapist at the bottom of page 117.

There is no right or wrong way to use this book. Whatever way you choose is exactly true for you.

I wish you the very best in your journey.

Charles L. Whitfield
Baltimore, November 1989

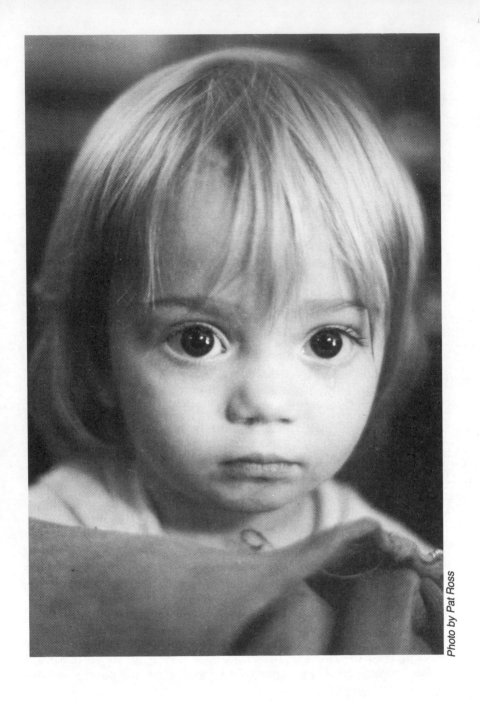

1

Getting Ready To Give Myself This Gift

Although mentioned since ancient times,
the concept of the "Child Within"
has been referred to and talked about
with increasing frequency
in the last decade.

Indeed, it has become the central healing
metaphor, principle and approach for
adult children of dysfunctional families
precisely because it is far more than a metaphor.

It is a *reality*.

Who Am I?

Our Child Within is who we really are
— ultimately alive, energetic, creative and fulfilled.

After we remove all the masks, facades,
trappings and superficialities of who
we may have thought we were
and who we may have needed to be to survive,
what remains is our True Self, our Real Self
— our Child Within.

But to survive a difficult childhood,
and for some people even a dangerous childhood
and adolescence, our Child Within went into hiding.
The pain and confusion was just too great for it.

Even though our Child Within
may have gone into hiding, it never dies.
It is always there, waiting
to peep its small head,
sometimes with big eyes, and
usually with an open heart,
out into life.

It wants to *be,* to experience,
to create, and evolve.
It wants to feel connected, to be a part of life,
the world, and the Universe.

When we discover and remember
this core of our identity,
we begin our healing journey and adventure.

There may be at least a million people
who have consciously started
this self-healing journey at this time.
And there are probably more than
200 times this number in this country
who are *un*-consciously seeking healing and fulfillment.

Virginia Satir, who created family therapy decades ago,
estimated that nearly all (about 95%) of families are dysfunctional.

A dysfunctional family is one in which *each member*
is not getting their needs met, and their psychological and spiritual
well-being and growth are not supported by the others.

And if you happen to have grown up
in such a troubled, unhealthy or dysfunctional family,
there is a way out of any associated unnecessary suffering.

In my book *Healing The Child Within,*
which I designed this workbook and guide
to accompany and to facilitate,
I describe four basic principles and actions
for this healing.

To rediscover our True or Real Self
and heal our Child Within,
we can begin a *process* that involves the following:

1) Discover and practice being our **Real Self** or Child Within.

2) Identify our **needs.**
   These needs are ongoing throughout our life and
   include our physical, mental, emotional and spiritual needs.
   And we practice getting these needs met
   alone, with safe and supportive people,
   and if we choose, with our Higher Power.

3) Identify, re-experience, and **grieve**
   the pain of our **ungrieved losses** or **traumas**
   in the presence of safe and supportive people.

4) Identify and work through our **core issues,**
   which I describe here, in *Healing the Child Within*
   and in a book in process called *Wisdom to Know the Difference.*

These actions are closely related, although not listed
in any particular order. Working on them, and thereby
healing our Child Within, generally occurs in a circular fashion
with work and discovery in one area being a link to another area.

Working in these four areas — with a progressively increasing
awareness and experience — constitutes the healing process.

Using this Book

I have created and designed this book
to facilitate that healing process.
Throughout its pages it includes **narrative,
guidelines** and **experiential exercises**
that can assist you in healing **your** Child Within.

Using this book in *any* way is entirely optional for you.
To start, you don't have to buy it.
And if you were to buy it, you could just read the material
and not do any of the exercises.
Another option is to try just one or two exercises.

Or you could slowly and carefully go through the book
and do whatever exercises you choose.
Finally, you could do more or even all of it,
taking your time not to rush through it.

To make this book work best for you, consider several components:

- **Risking** — to read, to do an exercise, to write in this book.

- **Reading** — this material and selected other books.

- **Reflecting** — on what is said or suggested and — on what comes up for *you* personally.

- **Considering** — your beliefs, thoughts, feelings and possibilities.

- **Experiencing** — your **inner life** in all its actual and potential richness, including its feelings and

- **Writing** — your thoughts and ideas, pain and joy, reactions and reflections — **anything** that comes up for you.

For those who feel some fear
or uneasiness or resistance to writing any of these things,
you can know that these feelings are just fine to have.
In healing our Child Within, we learn that all our feelings
are real and important.
Let them come up into your awareness.
Feel them.
When we let go and feel our feelings,
we may be breaking some of the rules
that we learned while growing up, e.g., "Don't feel."

Writing Things Down

Sometimes when an idea or an upset or a feeling comes up for us,
there is no one around who is safe who we can talk to.

So writing about it — just what that's like for us — is the next best
thing.

At **times** it can be even *more* helpful than talking to someone.

Research is showing that writing
these things down is not only **enlivening**
and **increases** our **self-awareness**,
but it also **strengthens** our body's **immune system**.
Through their study, research and experience,
people like Progoff, Pennebaker, Kritsberg and others —
and countless people who have done journaling
about their recovery and their lives,
or those who have kept a diary, have found
that writing things down has **helped** them
make their **life go better** —
including the gradual achievement of *more Success*
and *more Serenity.*

So, here is my offering to you.
As you choose to consider it, or not consider it,
to write some in it — or not,
it can become your **gift** to yourself.

Are you worthy of this kind of a gift?

If you're not sure, consider asking a
best friend or some trusted fellow travelers in recovery.
In recovery we learn that **we** have ultimate power
and choice in making our life go better.

No one else can do it for us.

Not even our
- Best friend
- Counselor
- Therapist
- Teacher
- Guru
- Mother
- Father
- Spouse
- Boyfriend or girlfriend
- Sponsor
- Doctor
- Clergy

— or any other   person.

If they are safe people, they can *help* us, *assist* us
and *be there* with us.

But we alone are responsible for our recovery now.

You Are Worthy

I wish you the best on this adventure and journey.

You — your Child Within, your Real or True Self —
are the captain, the worker, the creator, the experiencer
and the observer of your recovery and your life.
You are the writer, producer, director,
the star and the audience.
You are in charge!
If you choose, this experience can be

Your Gift to You.

This book is not just about writing things down.
It is about getting free, about recovery.
To get free, we begin to **identify** and **name** a lot of things,

I call this —

**The Power of Naming Things in Adult Child Recovery
Wherein I Name . . .**

Who I am	My Wants
	needs
What happened	similarities or sameness
	differentness or uniqueness
How I was mistreated	relationships
	addictions, attachments
My ungrieved hurts, losses	or compulsions
and traumas	
	My Core issues
Any toxic secrets	Basic dynamics
	(including boundaries & limits)
Any chronic distress	Dreams
	Goals
My Beliefs	
Thoughts	
Feelings	What is wrong
Possibilities	
Choices	What I want to happen
Experiences	How I can make that happen

To **name** things is **personal Power.**

Experiencing and **Choosing**

To get free, we also begin

to **EXPERIENCE** our lives

in progressively more and more authentic ways.

That is, **instead** of numbing or covering up our inner life
or distracting ourselves from it by all kinds of possible ways
(such as compulsive work, sex, television, eating, relationships,
gambling, exercise, alcohol, other drugs,
_____, _____ and _____, (fill in the blanks))

we choose to

EXPERIENCE

      our lives.

This experiencing includes all aspects
of our inner lives, including our *feelings,*
exactly *as they are happening*
in this moment. **Now.**

Sound difficult? — It is.
Sound confusing? — It is.
Sound simple? — It is.

To get free, we also begin

to **SHARE**

all of the above — what we *identify* and what we *experience* —
with *safe* others, with ourselves and, if we choose,
with our Higher Power.

This workbook and guidebook will help facilitate this exciting
and sacred journey and adventure of getting free — of recovery.

Just remember four simple words —

    It's always my choice.

You can always put this book down and take a rest.
Or you can throw it away. You may feel like doing
both of these at times.

The journey of recovery
is like the journey of life —

>   You can't do it alone.
>   And the only way
>   You can do it is alone.
>   . . . a paradox.

Are you uncomfortable with this paradox?
And with paradox in general?
If so, it shows that you're human. If you are
comfortable with it, perhaps you're an evolved spiritual being.
— Or perhaps you might not be fully aware of your feelings.
And that's just fine or you wouldn't need
to keep exploring and looking for answers.

There are many other guides and books that you can use
to supplement your healing process.
Throughout this book I will be referring
to four books (guess who wrote them?):

>   *Healing the Child Within:* Discovery and Recovery
>   for Adult Children of Dysfunctional Families.
>   *Wisdom to Know the Difference:* Transforming
>   Co-dependence into Healthy Relationships.
>   (working title of manuscript in process)
>   *Boundaries and Limits* in Relationships
>   and Recovery (working title)
>   and *Spirituality in Recovery.*

And there are several by other authors
that I'll be referring to as well.

While you won't need to own my four books
to use this workbook, it can *help* you
to use this workbook if you have read a copy
of *Healing the Child Within.*
But use your own judgment.
Nothing in this book —
like nothing in life — is a requirement.

This workbook and guidebook is set up
in sections of **brief discussions**
— like you've been reading —
and **exercises** for you to . . .

- Consider
- Risk doing
- Risk experiencing
- Risk sharing (if with a safe person) and
- Write about.

I will also offer some guidance
and suggestions about self-help groups,
group therapy, counseling and other aids
that you can use in healing your Child Within.

Because of the personal and confidential nature
of what you may write in this book,
you may choose not to leave it lying around
for just anyone to pick up.

After you have started writing in it, keep it in a safe place.*
To do this work, this *reading, reflecting* and *writing,*
I suggest that you be in a comfortable, safe, quiet place
with no distractions.

It is most healing to be able to focus on these words,
and especially on your inner life — including your beliefs, thoughts,
    feelings, decisions, choices and experiences
that you are having *right now,*
in this very moment.

— Quiet music can be okay for background.
Loud music, rock or fast-paced music, television
or conversation in the room or the next room
that might distract you in any way
may be detrimental to your healing process.
You may even consider unplugging your telephone
or simply "turn it over" to your answering machine.

---

*such as under your mattress
(unless you are a Princess or a Prince, sensitive to peas).

However you do it, you will usually begin
to heal best in a quiet, comfortable
and safe place, with no distractions.

Do you deserve it?

Are you worthy of this gift?

In the space below, if you choose, write any reactions
that you may be having to reading this first chapter.

2

Determining My
Recovery Potential

If you have read the first chapter
of *Healing the Child Within,**
you may have already partially completed this exercise.

If so, you can refer back to your answers there.

If not, for exercise number one, answer the following.

While not easy to determine whether you lean toward being
more healthy or less healthy in relationships with self and others,
you may find it helpful to answer some of the following questions.

I call it the "Recovery Potential Survey" because it reflects not
only our awareness of our woundedness, but also our potential
for growing and realizing an alive, adventurous and happy life.

---

*Hereafter, I'll refer to this book as *HCW.*

Recovery Potential Survey

Circle or check the word that most applies to how you *truly* feel.

1. Do you seek approval and affirmation?
   Never   Seldom   Occasionally   Often   Usually

2. Do you fail to recognize your accomplishments?
   Never   Seldom   Occasionally   Often   Usually

3. Do you fear criticism?
   Never   Seldom   Occasionally   Often   Usually

4. Do you overextend yourself?
   Never   Seldom   Occasionally   Often   Usually

5. Have you had problems with your own compulsive behavior?
   Never   Seldom   Occasionally   Often   Usually

6. Do you have a need for perfection?
   Never   Seldom   Occasionally   Often   Usually

7. Are you uneasy when your life is going smoothly?
   Do you continually anticipate problems?
   Never   Seldom   Occasionally   Often   Usually

8. Do you feel more alive in the midst of a crisis?
   Never   Seldom   Occasionally   Often   Usually

9. Do you care for others easily, yet find it difficult to care for yourself?
   Never   Seldom   Occasionally   Often   Usually

10. Do you isolate yourself from other people?
    Never   Seldom   Occasionally   Often   Usually

11. Do you respond with anxiety to authority figures and angry people?
    Never   Seldom   Occasionally   Often   Usually

12. Do you feel that individuals and society in general are taking advantage of you?
    Never   Seldom   Occasionally   Often   Usually

13. Do you have trouble with intimate relationships?
    Never   Seldom   Occasionally   Often   Usually

14. Do you attract and seek people who tend to be compulsive?
    Never   Seldom   Occasionally   Often   Usually

15. Do you cling to relationships because you are afraid of being alone?
    Never   Seldom   Occasionally   Often   Usually

16. Do you mistrust your own feelings and feelings expressed by others?
    Never   Seldom   Occasionally   Often   Usually

17. Do you find it difficult to express your emotions?
    Never   Seldom   Occasionally   Often   Usually

If you answered "Occasionally," "Often," or "Usually" to any of these questions, you may find it useful to continue reading. (These questions are modified from Al-Anon Family Group, 1984, with permission.)

18. Do you fear any of the following:
    Never   Seldom   Occasionally   Often   Usually
        • losing control?
    Never   Seldom   Occasionally   Often   Usually
        • your own feelings?
    Never   Seldom   Occasionally   Often   Usually
        • conflict and criticism?
    Never   Seldom   Occasionally   Often   Usually
        • being rejected or abandoned?
    Never   Seldom   Occasionally   Often   Usually
        • being a failure?
    Never   Seldom   Occasionally   Often   Usually

19. Is it difficult for you to relax and have fun?
    Never   Seldom   Occasionally   Often   Usually

20. Do you find yourself compulsively eating, working, drinking, using drugs or seeking excitement?
    Never   Seldom   Occasionally   Often   Usually

21. Have you tried counseling or psychotherapy, yet still feel that "something" is wrong or missing?
    Never   Seldom   Occasionally   Often   Usually

22. Do you frequently feel numb, empty or sad?
    Never   Seldom   Occasionally   Often   Usually

23. Is it hard for you to trust others?
    Never   Seldom   Occasionally   Often   Usually

24. Do you have an over-developed sense of responsibility?
    Never   Seldom   Occasionally   Often   Usually

25. Do you feel a lack of fulfillment in life, personally and in your work?
    Never   Seldom   Occasionally   Often   Usually

26. Do you have feelings of guilt, inadequacy or low self-esteem?
    Never   Seldom   Occasionally   Often   Usually

27. Do you have a tendency toward having chronic fatigue, aches and pains?
    Never   Seldom   Occasionally   Often   Usually

28. Do you find that it is difficult to visit your parents for more than a few minutes or a few hours?
    Never   Seldom   Occasionally   Often   Usually

29. Are you hesitant to respond when people ask about your feelings?
    Never   Seldom   Occasionally   Often   Usually

30. Have you wondered if you were mistreated or neglected as a child?
    Never   Seldom   Occasionally   Often   Usually

31. Do you have difficulty asking for what you want from others?
    Never   Seldom   Occasionally   Often   Usually

If you answered "Occasionally," "Often," or "Usually" to any of these questions, this book may be helpful to you. If you answered mostly "Never," you may not be aware of some of your feelings.

Of **your above answers,** which are the issues
that you might need to work on *especially* in your healing process?
To help clarify these, **write in the space below**
a list or a summary of the items that you marked as **Usually.**

Write in the space below
a summary of the items that you marked as **Often.**

These above observations, issues or concerns are ones that
you might need to be **especially** aware of as you go through
your **healing** process.

Next, **write in the space below**
a summary of the items that you marked as **Occasionally.**
These are issues that you might **consider**
and **look for** in your recovery process.

Finally, **write in the space below**
a summary of the items that you marked as **Never.**

While these may actually be true for you,
sometimes people who check these as **Never**
are not fully aware of some of these being issues in their life.

When a person marks **Seldom,** the issue is not usually a problem
for them.

Would you like to **take a break** now?
   If so, use a mark to remember where you left off.

Now take a few minutes
and reflect back on all of these issues or observations.

As you do, you might wish to **underline**
whichever observations or issues are
of *most concern for you in your life right now.*

On the next page, or in your personal diary
or journal, you might consider writing this issue
or issues at the top of the page, and then,
if you have time, writing freely about it.

Some helpful areas or questions to consider
when writing each issue may include:

- What is **your own definition** of the issue or item?

- How has it or does it **come up for you in your life**?

- How did it **come up when** you were a **child**?

- How does it fit in or affect your **relationships**?

- How might it be related to any of your
  addictions, attachments or **compulsions**?

- How might it be related to your **feelings**?

- What else?

- Any ideas on **how** you could **work through**
  this issue?

- Do you feel **safe** enough to **share any** of this
  with a trusted person?

Remember, this book is for your eyes only,
unless you choose to show it to someone.

You don't need to get it perfect!

Notes on Issues of Most Concern to Me Right Now

My Personal Strengths and Resources

Begin to reflect on your personal strengths and resources that you have now that can help you in your healing. Consider those that may be **internal** — e.g. desire, motivation, imagination, openness to recovery issues and any associated feelings. Also consider any **external** strengths — e.g. support groups, friends, counselor or therapist, therapy group, trusted family and the like. Feel free to list any of these in the space below.

Congratulations!

You are already healing your Child Within.

As you continue to heal your Child Within,
you will likely find it helpful
to refer back to these items or issues.

You might want to get a notebook
or diary to do additional writing,
such as the kind you've just done above.
And remember to store it in a safe place.

Would you like to **take a break** now?

I recommend a fairly long amount
of time between each of these exercises
— *at least* a week — or even longer.

That little Child may need the time
to develop the trust it will need
before it can begin to come out.

So give it as much time as it needs.

Then continue with the next section,
whenever that might feel right for you.

3

Who Am I?

Since our True Self went into hiding
and our false self then had to run the show,
it may be hard to know
who we really are.

This is an exercise in getting to know ourself.

This experiential chapter is in four parts.

Part One is for you to do alone,
again in a quiet, comfortable and safe place.

It includes a list of incomplete sentences
about yourself. **Section A** is about who you **really** are,
Section B is about who you may **pretend** to be.

Don't think too long or too hard for your answer.
The most honest and accurate one
often pops up without much
or even any particular thought.

Know that this exercise and these words are for your eyes
— your Child Within's eyes — only.
They are not for anyone else to see.
This part usually takes about 20 to 30 minutes.
So whenever the time and place are right for you, feel free to start.
There are no right or wrong answers,
only answers which may reveal our True Self or our false self.

Part One

Section A: Phrases to help trigger **my reflection on**

Who I Really Am

Please complete the following honestly.

I am . . .
The main thing about me is . . .

I always . . .
I feel most like me when . . .

What I like most about a person is . . .

I will be . . .
I get angry when . . .
I feel happiest when . . .

I believe in . . .
One thing I want to accomplish is . . .

What I like most about myself is . . .

I hate it when . . .
I was . . .
I feel least like me when . . .

If you really knew me . . .
I feel weakest when . . .
When I feel angry, I . . .
On a rainy day I like to . . .

I feel good when I remember . . .

When I'm alone I feel . . .
Most of all I really want . . .
I was the type of child who . . .
One thing I'd like to change about myself is . . .

I feel strongest when . . .
On a beautiful day I like to . . .
My favorite pastime is . . .
When I feel happy, I like to . . .
If my relationship with _____ were to end, . . .

My Child Within is . . .

Section B: Phrases to help trigger **my reflection on**

Who I Pretend To Be

Please complete the following honestly.

I pretend to be . . .

Most people don't know that I . . .

I give the impression of . . .

The mask I wear is . . .

On the surface I am . . .

The game I play is . . .

I hide behind . . .

I wear makeup because . . .

The clothes I wear indicate . . .

The car I drive shows that . . .

My job or profession shows others that . . .

The real me hides under . . .

How long I've been pretending is . . .

How often I pretend is . . .

That was **Part One**.

Part Two involves finding a safe person,
who you trust, one who will keep a confidence.
(See Chapter 5 for details on safe and unsafe people.)
It is optional for that person to have also
completed part one. If they did,
you can do this as a *reciprocal* exercise.
If not, do it with just **you** doing the following.

Tell them in your own words
— not necessarily what you wrote in part one,
although it's okay to refer to it anytime —
first, who you really are.

Take as long as you need.

Then, tell them who you pretend to be.

Take as long as you need.

After completing Part Two, if you want, you can
take a break now for from a few minutes to a few hours.

Then go on to Part Three.

Part Three of this four-part exercise is reflecting back on
Parts One and **Two**.

Ask yourself, "What was **that experience like** for me?"

"What **feelings** came up for me?"

"What did I **learn** from doing them?"

In the space below, **write anything that comes up**
for you as you reflect on these questions.

The final part,
Part Four, is **ongoing** and will require
little effort on your part.

Whenever anything in your inner life comes up
about these questions
"Who am I?" and
"Who do I pretend to be?"
just reflect on them.
Consider them.
As these experiences from your inner life
come up, you might pause
and let yourself **feel** and **experience** them
as **completely** as possible, right in that moment,
just as they are coming up for you.

Some further options include

• **Writing** them down
   either here or in your diary or journal and

• **Sharing** your experiences with a safe person.

To facilitate this reflection as **Part Four,**
I have reproduced a poem on the next page that
the author gave me permission to print here and in *HCW.*

Use the space below to write whatever comes up for you.

Please Hear What I'm Not Saying

Don't be fooled by me.
Don't be fooled by the face I wear.
For I wear a mask, a thousand masks,
masks that I'm afraid to take off,
and none of them is me.
Pretending is an art that's second nature with me,
but don't be fooled.
For God's sake don't be fooled.
I give you the impression that I'm secure,
that all is sunny and unruffled with me, within as well
    as without,
that confidence is my name and coolness my game,
that the water's calm and I'm in command,
and that I need no one.
But don't believe me.
My surface may seem smooth but my surface is my mask,
ever-varying and ever-concealing.
Beneath lies no complacence.
Beneath lies confusion and fear and aloneness.
But I hide this. I don't want anybody to know it.

I panic at the thought of my weakness and fear
    being exposed.
That's why I frantically create a mask to hide behind,
a nonchalant sophisticated facade,
to help me pretend,
to shield me from the glance that knows.
But such a glance is precisely my salvation.
    My only hope and I know it.
That is, if it's followed by acceptance,
if it's followed by love.
It's the only thing that can liberate me from myself,
from my own self-built prison walls,
from the barriers I so painstakingly erect.
It's the only thing that will assure me of what I can't
    assure myself,
that I'm really worth something.

But I don't tell you this. I don't dare. I'm afraid to.
I'm afraid your glance will not be followed by acceptance,
will not be followed by love.
I'm afraid you'll think less of me, that you'll laugh,
and your laugh would kill me.
I'm afraid that deep-down I'm nothing, that I'm just
     no good,
and that you will see this and reject me.

So I play my game, my desperate pretending game,
with a facade of assurance without
and a trembling child within.
So begins the glittering but empty parade of masks,
and my life becomes a front.
I idly chatter to you in the suave tones of surface talk.
I tell you everything that's really nothing,
and nothing of what's everything,
of what's crying within me.
So when I'm going through my routine,
do not be fooled by what I'm saying.
Please listen carefully and try to hear what I'm not saying,
what I'd like to be able to say,
what for survival I need to say,
but what I can't say.

I don't like to hide.
I don't like to play superficial phony games.
I want to stop playing them.
I want to be genuine and spontaneous and me,
but you've got to help me.
You've got to hold out your hand
even when that's the last thing I seem to want.
Only you can wipe away from my eyes the blank stare of the
     breathing dead.
Only you can call me into aliveness.
Each time you're kind and gentle and encouraging,
each time you try to understand because you really care,
my heart begins to grow wings,
very small wings,

very feeble wings,
but wings!
With your power to touch me into feeling
you can breathe life into me.
I want you to know that.

I want you to know how important you are to me,
how you can be a creator — a honest-to-God creator —
of the person that is me
if you choose to.
You alone can break down the wall behind which I tremble,
you alone can remove my mask,
you alone can release me from my shadow-world of panic
    and uncertainty, from my lonely prison,
if you choose to.
Please choose to. Do not pass me by.
It will not be easy for you.

A long conviction of worthlessness builds strong walls.
The nearer you approach to me,
the blinder I may strike back.
It's irrational, but despite what the books say about man,
often I am irrational.
I fight against the very thing that I cry out for.
But I am told that love is stronger than strong walls,
and in this lies my hope.
Please try to beat down those walls
with firm hands
but with gentle hands
for a child is very sensitive.

Who am I, you may wonder?
I am someone you know very well.
For I am every man you meet
and I am every woman you meet.

Charles C. Finn

26

4

Getting My Needs Met

From the second we are born
we have needs.
These needs are healthy and normal.

In a healthy family the parents are able
to get their own needs met in a healthy way,
and able to help and support one another
in getting these met. Thus they are
capable and free to provide for
the child's needs. They also model
and help the child in getting its own needs met.

The more wounded the parents are
and the more troubled, unhealthy
or dysfunctional the family is,
the less the child will be able to
get its needs met by parents and even by itself.
The child becomes so preoccupied
with others' behavior and needs
that it is unable to get many or even most
of its own needs met.
Unable to get its needs met,
and feeling increasingly overwhelmed with pain
— who we really are — our Child Within, our True Self —
goes into hiding.

What emerges to *help it survive*
is a false self, a co-dependent self.

The Child Goes Into Hiding

Suzette Billedeaux

Other than assisting with survival, this false self
is incapable of getting our needs met.

Our Child still has needs,
and from time to time it will peep out
or even bust out to try to get some of them met.
At times this busting out occurs through
an unhealthy explosion or
a binge of an addiction or a compulsion
and may end up hurting us or hurting another.

So, how do we learn to get our needs met?
First, we can **find out** what our **needs are**.

Take a few minutes now
and consider what **your own needs** are.
As each of these needs comes to mind, **write** them in the
space below. Take your time in considering and writing these.

Ideally, our needs must be met so that our Child Within
can develop and grow and be creative and feel alive.

How many of these needs did you get met as a child?
How many as an adolescent? How many as an adult?
During each of these times, **how** did you get these met?
Take a few minutes to **reflect on** these questions.

On the next two pages, as **Part A** of this exercise,
I have listed our healthy human needs
in a column along the left side of the page.
Across the page are blank spaces for you
to **reflect upon** and fill in with your personal answers
to these questions.

As a *child* and an *adolescent* —

- Did you get your needs **met**?

- If so, **how** did you get them met?

- Were any of the ways **unhealthy** or **unsafe**?

Take as much time as you need to reflect upon these
and to write your answers.

Remember, there are **no wrong answers**.
What comes up for you is always true for you.

Table 4.1. Part A: As a Child and Adolescent

Need	Did you get need met? (Yes or No?)	How did you get need met?

1. Survival
2. Safety

3. Touching, skin contact
4. Attention
5. Mirroring and echoing

6. Guidance
7. Listening

8. Being real

9. Participating
10. Acceptance
    Others are aware of, take seriously
        and admire the Real You
    Freedom to be the Real You
    Tolerance of your feelings
    Validation
    Respect
    Belonging and love

11. Opportunity to grieve losses and to grow

12. Support
13. Loyalty and trust
14. Accomplishment
    Mastery, "Power," "Control"
    Creativity
    Having a sense of completion
    Making a contribution
15. Altering one's state of consciousness,
        transcending the ordinary
16. Sexuality

17. Enjoyment or fun
18. Freedom

19. Nurturing

20. Unconditional love (including connection with a Higher Power)

These are a list of healthy human needs. They start with the most primitive and simple, and end with the more sophisticated and complex.

Were any of these ways **unhealthy** or **unsafe**? (Describe)

Table 4.2. Part B: Think of Yourself *Today*

Need	Are You Getting Each Need Met? (Yes or No?)	How?
1. Survival		
2. Safety		
3. Touching, skin contact		
4. Attention		
5. Mirroring and echoing		
6. Guidance		
7. Listening		
8. Being real		
9. Participating		

10. Acceptance
    Others are aware of, take seriously
      and admire the Real You
    Freedom to be the Real You
    Tolerance of your feelings
    Validation
    Respect
    Belonging and love		

11. Opportunity to grieve losses and to grow		
12. Support		
13. Loyalty and trust		

14. Accomplishment
    Mastery, "Power," "Control"
    Creativity
    Having a sense of completion
    Making a contribution		

15. Altering one's state of consciousness, transcending the ordinary		
16. Sexuality		
17. Enjoyment or fun		
18. Freedom		
19. Nurturing		
20. Unconditional love (including connection with a Higher Power)		

If not, **how might** you do so healthily and safely?

Doing this exercise might take you a long time.
You do **not** need to hurry. There is absolutely **no rush**.

Did you ever feel rushed as a child?

You don't have to rush now.
This is your private book.
And your private and personal healing and recovery.

There is no one telling you to do anything.
It is always your individual choice.
In fact, if you feel overwhelmed by or even
bored with this chapter or **any** part of this book,
what are your **choices**?

In writing this book, my own choices included:

- Continue writing
- Continue reading (what I'd just written)
- Think about what I want to write
- Daydream
- Reflect back on a previous page
- Focus on my inner life and my feelings (at times hard to do)
- Feel my feelings (sometimes the hardest)
- Remember
- Take a break
- Do something else
- Talk to a safe person about any of this
- Anything else I wanted or needed to do

Possibilities and Choices give us **freedom** from the limiting, isolating and numbing of all-or-none thinking, feeling and behaving.
So, if you choose, consider your possibilities and your choices.

One is to **write** in any choices you might have now, or anytime, on a blank sheet of paper or in your diary.

If you haven't taken a break from working on your healing in this chapter, you might consider taking one now. As you take this break, you may be more aware of your needs throughout your daily life. After your break, reflect back on what it was like to do this exercise. Write any comments or reflections in your diary or journal.

5

Who Is Safe To Talk To?

In *Healing the Child Within* and in this book
I've mentioned several times that we can help
heal ourself by talking to safe people.

But how can I know if someone is safe?

I may have trusted some people in my past
and they ended up hurting me.

So how can I really tell?

My experience is that there is no 100% sure way
to tell without experimenting, trial and error
or share-check-share (Gravitz & Bowden, 1985).

I have found some guidelines, though,
which I discuss in *Wisdom to Know the Difference,*
and in *Boundaries And Limits in Relationships And Recovery.*
For your consideration, I list them on the next page.

Table 5.1. Some Characteristics of Safe and Unsafe People

Safe	Unsafe
Listen to you	Don't listen
Hear you	Don't hear
Make eye contact	No eye contact
Accept the real you	Reject the real you
Validate the real you	Invalidate the real you
Nonjudgmental	Judgmental
Are real with you	False with you
Clear	Unclear
Boundaries appropriate and clear	Boundaries unclear, messages mixed
Direct	Indirect
No triangles	Triangle - in others
Supportive	Competitive
Loyal	Betray
Relationship authentic	Relationship feels contrived

Not all of these characteristics are absolute. For example, some people who make eye contact, listen to you and are supportive may still be unsafe. And a safe person may be unclear at times. However, over time, these characteristics and others may be helpful in differentiating who is safe from who is unsafe.

Have you met anyone who feels safe to you?

Do you know anyone *now* who feels safe?

If you have a few minutes,
reflect on who you knew in the past
and on who you know now.

Include anyone who comes up in your awareness.
Family. Friends. Acquaintances. Enemies. Sponsor(s).
Therapist(s). Counselor(s). Clergy.
Other helping professionals. Anyone.
Of these people, who has felt safe or feels safe to you now?

In the space at the top of the next page,
write in either the names, initials, description or a code word
for anyone who felt or who feels safe to you now.

Safe People In My Life

From My Past | **In My Present**

Remember, this is your private journal, so what you write in it is for your eyes only. If you feel reluctant to write a person's name here, you can use a code or write it on a piece of paper or in your diary or journal and keep it in a safe place.

Next, list any unsafe people in your life in the space below.

Unsafe People In My Life

From My Past | **In My Present**

Take your time with these exercises.

When you come to a point where
you feel that you've about completed
your list of **safe** people, consider the following.

Pick **one** person on that list, perhaps the safest.
Meet with them in person and tell them
how and why you feel safe with them.
(If they are too far away, you might consider calling them.)

What was it like to do that exercise?
What was it like to share what you did with your safest person?
What feelings came up or are coming up for you now?

In the space below, write your answers to these questions,
and/or write whatever is coming up for you right now.

Take as much time and space as you need.

We can heal our Child Within

in three relationships

— with our self alone, with safe others

and, if we choose, with our Higher Power.

We have been talking about safety with others.

Is my Child Within safe with *me*?

The answer may come slowly.

As you get to know your Child better,
and as it gets to know you,
you may begin to discover that
you **are** your Child Within, your True Self.

Is my Child Within safe with my Higher Power?

This also is an answer that is
completely personal and only you know,
or will come to know, the answer.

Think about your answers to these questions.

When you have time, write whatever comes up
for you in the space below or in your journal.

Notes

6

What Happened?

On page 6, I introduced the importance
of **naming** things in — and about —
our life and our recovery.

Giving a name to these
facilitates our healing.

High on that list of things to name are
what happened and what might have been
our **ungrieved hurts, losses and traumas**.

Finding out what happened usually
unfolds **gradually** and is often painful.
It usually comes in *waves*
and in *fits* and *starts*.
And it may take a *long time*
— so give yourself plenty of time.
Take all the time you need.

Discovering what happened is often painful
and we naturally want the pain to pass.

This is where the gift to ourself of *patience*
can be so helpful.

By the time you read this you may already know some —
or even a lot — about what happened to you.

By *what happened* I mean, first of all,
how we may have become **wounded**.
In helping people to heal themselves —
to heal their Child Within —
I prefer to use the term *wounded*
rather than a label or diagnosis
that often translates to a number of people,
including us, as "bad," "sick," "crazy," or "stupid."
The truth is that we are none of those.

What happened possibly was that
we didn't get the healthy parenting
we needed. We may have even been *mistreated*.
And so **our reaction** to that — as a Child — was not our fault.
As a child, our reaction was simply a **normal** reaction
to an unhealthy situation.

It was an otherwise healthy reaction that allowed us to survive,
one that protected that vulnerable little Child inside of us.

To begin to discover and to describe what happened,
it can be helpful to take a look at the family in which we grew up.

My Family Tree

One useful exercise in healing our Child
is making our family tree.
On page 44 is a diagram with a lot of circles,
each of which may represent a member of your family.
Starting with yourself, inside the circle write the name,
the age and in it or next to it
write any outstanding or memorable
characteristics of that person.

Because we are becoming more and more knowledgeable
about conditions that can exist in people, and because
some people are breaking the "no talk" rule nowadays,
we may **know** whether someone has
an illness or condition that may have
rendered them dysfunctional (i.e., to **us** they were and/or are
unable to be a healthy parent, sibling, grandparent,
aunt, uncle, child or other relative, etc.).

For more detailed approaches to the family tree or genogram, see McGoldrick & Gerson,
1985.

Some of these conditions may include
alcoholism (Alcsm), another chemical dependence (CD),
adult child (AC), compulsive gambling (CG), workaholism (Wksm),
sexual addiction (SA), co-dependence (Co-dep),
rage - aholism (Rgsm), religious addiction (RA) or
strict religious (SR), verbal abuse (VA),
violence or physical abuse (Viol), incest (In),
cancer (Ca), other physical illness (PI), mental illness (MI),
suicide (SU), an eating disorder (ED), or nicotine dependence (ND).

On the next three pages after the family tree are definitions of these conditions.

When making your family tree, use these
abbreviations if there is not enough room to write
all the words that apply to each member.
As an example, I show a completed family
tree in Appendix 1 (p. 261) at the back of this book.
You can make a blow-up of the next page for more space.

Take as much time as you need to fill out this family tree.
You may need to do some detective work
over the next few months **or even longer**
to discreetly discover just what happened
for some of these family members.

A caution: you may choose **not** to tell
whomever you are speaking to about any of this, that you
are making a family tree, or *anything*
about your recovery. Some family members
may not be safe for you to self-disclose with
about these often delicate matters.

To help you remember who on your family tree
is not complete, write their names in the space below.
When your information is complete with them,
write it in on your family tree.

When you have written in all you know for now about
your family, take a break from this work for a few days.

Starting with yourself, write the name and the age inside the circle and in it or next to it write any outstanding or memorable characteristics of that person. Use any of the following abbreviations:

Alcsm = Alcoholism	Co-dep = Co-dependent	In = Incest
CD = other Chemical Dependence	RA = Religious Addiction	Ca = Cancer
AC = Adult Child	SR = Strict Religious	MI = Mental Illness
CG = Compulsive Gambler	ED = Eating Disorder	Su = Suicide
Wksm = Workaholism	DF = Dysfunctional Family	Rec = Recovering
Viol = Violence or physical abuse	ND = Nicotine Dependence	VA = Verbal Abuse
SA = Sexual Addiction	Rgsm = Rage-aholism	PI = Physical Illness

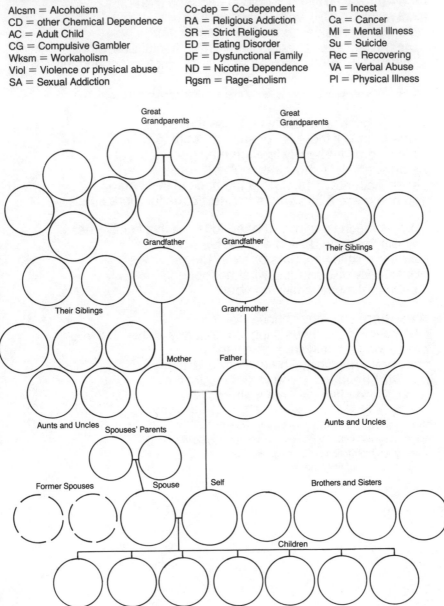

Figure 6.1. My Family Tree

To begin defining some of these conditions,
I offer the following brief descriptions.

Co-dependence — Suffering and dysfunction associated with
or due to focusing on the needs or behaviors of others.
Unless a family member is well into a full recovery program
(described later) all members of troubled families
are co-dependent to some degree.

Chemical dependence — Recurring trouble
associated with drinking or using other drugs.
The trouble may be in any one or more
of several life areas: physical, mental,
emotional, spiritual, relationships, job, legal and financial.
If you are uncertain about someone's drinking or drug use,
you may take the Family Drinking Survey in Appendix 2 (p. 253).

Compulsive gambling — Recurring trouble
associated with betting, gambling, investing
or financially risking in any way. The trouble
may be in any of the areas under CD above.

Workaholism — Working to the detriment
of our relationship with ourself or with others,
especially family or other close people.
Like co-dependence, this addiction is endemic
or common in our world.

Sexual addiction — Sexual activity of *any kind,*
including repeated fantasizing, that recurringly interferes
with or substitutes for our relationship with
ourself or with others, including our spouse.

Rage-aholism — Recurring use of fits of
anger or rage to control, manipulate or avoid
authentic relationship with self and others.

Verbal abuse — Any demeaning, shaming, judging
or put-down used to avoid authentic
relationship with self and others.

Violence or physical abuse — Physical
lashing out or attacking of any kind,
usually with the intent to control or harm another.

Religious addiction — A recurring pattern of
using religion in any one or a combination of ways:
judgmentalism, righteousness, rigidity or as a way
to alter one's state of consciousness, usually
used unconsciously, to avoid our authentic relationship with our
self, others and our Higher Power.

Eating disorder — A recurring pattern of any one or
a combination of: overeating, binging, purging, not eating
or overeating-alternating-with-dieting-or-compulsive-exercising,
usually used to unconsciously avoid authentic relationship
with self, others or Higher Power.

Incest or Sexual abuse — Any inappropriate talking, flirting or
touching or any fondling or other sexual activity
with any family member or step-members.
It is usually done by a person who is
one-up or in a position of power
to a person who is one-down or vulnerable.

Mental illness — May be mistaken for or associated with any
of the above. Any mental or emotional disorder,
whether or not the person ever recovered
or received "treatment" for it. Our accumulating
knowledge of adult child wounding, co-dependence,
the addictions, recovery and healing our
Child Within may stimulate us to re-think
the entire notion of "mental illness."

If you want further clarification of any of these or other
conditions, you can consult any of the references or
talk to someone with expertise in the specific condition.

The point of using these definitions is **not**
to take another person's "inventory,"
or to accuse or blame them.
The point is simply to *begin describing*
for yourself **what happened**.

Using My Family Tree

Now that I have started to fill in my family tree,
how might I begin to use it in my healing?

Remember — healing and recovery are in part discovering
progressively and using **increasing possibilities** and **choices**.
These possibilities and choices are most healing
if **you** discover and create them **yourself**.
When you do that, they are **yours to keep forever**.
(. . . Unless you choose to **dis**create any of them
and discover and create **new** possibilities and choices.)

Before looking at the next page, in the space below,
write just how you might imagine *using* the information in your
family tree.

Here are some ways that I can imagine
using the information and insights from my family tree.

1. Discovering **who** in my family
   may have been **dysfunctional** or **troubled**,
   and how or why they might have been so.

2. Seeing how they were then **unable to be** a
   healthy father, mother, brother, sister, aunt,
   uncle, grandmother, grandfather, step-relative, etc., to me.

3. Seeing how I **didn't get** my **needs** met as a child.

4. Beginning to **see more clearly** why my Child Within
   needed to go into **hiding** to survive.

5. As a part of my healing, **sharing** this information
   with trusted and safe others, such as my:

   • Best friend (if they are not in denial about their family)
   • Counselor or therapist
   • Self-help group (if Adult Children or Co-dependents
     Anonymous)
   • Therapy group
   • Sponsor (if in Adult Children or Co-dependents Anonymous)

6. **Facilitating my grieving** of the hurts, losses or traumas
   that I experienced, but that I never got to grieve and complete.

Are any feelings, confusion or insights coming up for you now?
If so, you might want to **write about them** here and in your
diary or journal.

When you are finished, take a break from this work for a few days.
Use safe people for support if pain comes up for you.

7

What Else Happened?

I mentioned earlier (page 6) that
to get free, we can begin to **identify** and to **name**
a lot of things that have happened,
things that we have experienced,
or may even only have partially experienced.

So, from your base knowledge now
about your family background or family tree,
let's begin to explore some more.

We know that our Child Within
goes into hiding for some real and important reasons:

- It isn't allowed to be and to express itself

- It hurts so bad

- It doesn't think it can survive otherwise, and

- No one in the family models
  any other way out for it.

For our Child Within to go into hiding,
there has to be some serious trouble, illness
and/or dysfunction in other family members.
You may have identified some of these
in your family tree.

To survive and to cope,
the Child does two more key things —

1. It takes in or internalizes negative messages
   about itself, and it often takes the blame
   for whatever goes wrong in the family
   and
2. It idealizes its parents.

This idealizing protects it from the otherwise overwhelming fact
that its parents are unhealthy and inadequate as parents.

And if that were true, it would have to face
the pain of that reality, and it feels like it might not survive.

If you have some time now,
make yourself comfortable in a quiet place.
Arrange your environment so that you
will not be interrupted for the next hour or so.

Begin to reflect back on your past.

Take your time.

Think of what some of the reasons
might have been for your Child to go into hiding.

How was it mistreated, abused or hurt?

In the spaces on the next pages,
write anything that comes up for you regarding
how you may have been mistreated, abused or hurt.

Remember, our purpose is not to blame anyone.

Our purpose here, in **healing** our Child Within,
is to continue to **name** what happened.

So, perhaps mustering up some courage,
write **anything** that comes up for you about
what happened —
how you might have been mistreated, abused
or hurt by **anyone** in your past,
starting with your **childhood**.
Include your **adolescence** and, if you choose,
your **adult** life up until now.

To facilitate your remembering, I have divided
the headings into the following areas of
our life: Physical, Mental, Emotional and Spiritual.

PHYSICAL Mistreatments, Abuses or Hurts

MENTAL Mistreatments, Abuses or Hurts

EMOTIONAL Mistreatments, Abuses or Hurts

SPIRITUAL Mistreatments, Abuses or Hurts

To help you begin to **name** what happened
I have listed on the next page some terms
for mistreatments, abuse or hurts
reproduced from Table 5, page 40 from *HCW.*

Table 7.1. Some Terms for Physical, Mental, Emotional and Spiritual Trauma That May Be Experienced by Children and Adults.

Abandonment
Neglect
Abuse: Physical — spanking, beating, torture, sexual, etc.
　　　　Mental — covert sexual (e.g., flirting, seducing)
　　　　Emotional — (see below)
　　　　Spiritual — (see below and text)

Shaming
Humiliating
Degrading
Inflicting guilt
Criticizing
Disgracing
Joking about
Laughing at
Teasing
Manipulating
Deceiving
Tricking
Betraying
Hurting
Being Cruel
Belittling
Intimidating
Patronizing
Threatening
Inflicting fear
Overpowering or bullying
Controlling

Limiting
Withdrawing/
Withholding love
Not taking seriously
Invalidating
Discrediting
Misleading
Disapproving
Making light of or minimizing
　　your feelings, wants or needs
Breaking promises
Raising hopes falsely
Responding inconsistently or
　　arbitrarily
Making vague demands
Stifling
Saying "you shouldn't . . . feel
　　such and such, e.g., anger"
Saying "If only . . . e.g., you were
　　better or different" or
"You should . . . e.g., be better
　　or different" (See also negative
　　messages in Table 8.1)

This exercise, remembering what else happened,
may take a long time.
Also helpful to facilitate what happened is to . . .

- Talk to your therapist or counselor about any of this.
- Attend some Adult Children Anonymous self-help meetings and
- Read or reread Chapters 4 through 7 of *Healing the Child Within*.

Like other exercises in this book, you might find it useful to return to this one more than once. If you choose, I encourage you to do that.

After you have worked as much as you want on this exercise, it can be healing for you to take a break from it.

<u>Notes</u>

If working through any of this material in any part of this book gets to be too painful or confusing for you, I suggest that you contact a professional therapist for a consultation (see page 130), and that you slow down on your use of this material.

8

Did I Learn Any Rigid Rules Or Negative Messages?

As we heal ourself, there are other things
that we can remember about **what happened.**

Two of these are the *rigid rules* and *negative messages*
that we were taught and that we learned to believe about ourselves.

One of the ways that troubled families are dysfunctional is by
the parents' or other parent figures' creation of **rigid rules**.

In an attempt to survive, the Child incorporates these rigid rules
into its subconscious mind, where they can remain
and create pain for it — until it begins its healing in some way.

In the space below and on to the next page, write any **rigid rules**
that you may remember from your family.

Rigid Rules That I Learned

Another way that troubled families
are dysfunctional is that they deliver
negative messages to the Child about itself.
Like the rigid rules, the Child — idealizing the parents —
incorporates these negative self-messages
into its subconscious mind
where they can remain as unalterable beliefs,
until it begins healing itself in some way.
Did you believe any of these negative messages
about yourself? Do you **still** believe any of them?
Think about some of these negative messages,
and in the space below, write any
that you might remember.

Negative Messages That I Learned

Because we learned many of these rules
and messages unconsciously
— outside of our ordinary awareness —
and because we might store many of them
in our unconscious mind,
remembering them can be difficult.
So in this process of remembering, take your time.
Simply doing these exercises may trigger new memories, too.

To assist your remembering, I list below
some negative rules and messages commonly
heard in troubled families (from Table 6, page 47 of *HCW*).

Table 8.1. Negative Rules and Negative Messages Commonly Heard in Alcoholic or Other Troubled Families

Negative Rules	Negative Messages
Don't express your feelings	Shame on you
Don't get angry	You're not good enough
Don't get upset	I wish I'd never had you
Don't cry	Your needs are not all right with me
Do as I say, not as I do	
Be good, "nice," perfect	Hurry up and grow up
Avoid conflict (or avoid dealing with conflict)	Be dependent
	Be a man
Don't think or talk; just follow directions	Big boys don't cry
	Act like a nice girl (or a lady)
Do well in school	You don't feel that way
Don't ask questions	Don't be like that
Don't betray the family	You're so stupid (or bad, etc.)
Don't discuss the family with outsiders; keep the family secret	You caused it
	You owe it to us
Be seen and not heard!	Of course we love you!
No back talk	I'm sacrificing myself for you
Don't contradict me	How can you do this to me?
Always look good	We won't love you if you . . .
I'm always right, you're always wrong	You're driving me crazy!
	You'll never accomplish anything
Always be in control	It didn't really hurt
Focus on the alcoholic's drinking (or troubled person's behavior)	You're so selfish
	You'll be the death of me yet
Drinking (or other troubled behavior) is not the cause of our problems	That's not true
	I promise (though breaks it)
	You make me sick
Always maintain the status quo	We wanted a boy/girl
Everyone in the family must be an enabler	You _____
	(fill in the blank)

Take as much time as you need to work on this chapter.
You can return to it and add to it whenever you remember
another rigid rule or negative message.

Also consider the following:

This, plus what you discovered in the prior two chapters,
is what you were taught
and what you learned about family,
relationships and yourself.

And furthermore:

It was not your fault!
You didn't cause it.

Is that possible?

The space below is for you to begin writing any
reflections on any of the above. How does any of this
affect you now in your relationships with yourself,
others and, if you choose, with your Higher Power?

There are some ways to begin to change and to reprogram these rigid rules and negative
messages (see the rest of this book, including Chapter 25). When we use these
techniques, we are healing our Child Within. Talking to a safe person about all this can help.

9

My Feelings

Throughout this book, just like when I assist people
in therapy, I talk about the healing power
of our **inner life**. A major part of our **inner life** is our

Feelings

When we are outer focused to the detriment
of our True Self, our Child Within,
we are fragmented, crippled and co-dependent.

Because our childhood was so difficult,
we had to shut out large parts of our inner life
in order to survive. We also may have had
few healthy role models to teach us about life.

And most of our peers and the rest of society
were in the same boat, only we and they didn't know it.
We may have learned certain rigid rules and negative messages
about feelings, such as, "Don't feel," "Don't get angry,"
"Only Daddy or Mommy can get angry," and
"Your feelings are not important."

In discovering and healing our True Self, we learn
that many of those old rules and messages are not true,
and we begin to become more and more aware
of that powerful part of us: our **inner life**,
and its major component — **our Feelings**.
Take a few minutes now, go inside yourself
and see, sense or feel what is happening.
What feelings are you feeling right now?
Write these in your journal or on a sheet of paper, or below.

Throughout this book I have talked of the importance
of **naming** things (see especially pages 6 and 50.)
As we **name** our feelings — each feeling —
we begin to heal. That is why I asked the previous question
and why I suggested writing down your feelings.
When we speak it and write it, we usually thereby give it a name.

But many adult children and co-dependent people
are not used to feeling their feelings completely,
so it may be hard to give some of them names.
Or they may be so indoctrinated by society,
including some influence from the fields of psychology
and psychiatry,
that they give certain feelings names that are not accurate.
Such as calling a feeling —

Depression	when it is actually	**Sadness**
Anxiety	when it is actually	**Fear**
Resentment	when it is actually	**Anger**
	or	
"High"	when it is actually	**Joy**

These words may not be wrong, but they are
just off the mark enough that as names they further contribute
to our confusion about and alienation from our feelings.

It can take a *long time* to learn
a more accurate and useful language of feelings.
I have suggested that in the best full recovery program
this long time is usually from three to five years or more.

So give yourself plenty of time to begin to learn, and then to learn
more and more about this new language.
As you heal, you may return
to this chapter several more times over the coming months
and years, and return to some of the other chapters in this book
and in *Healing the Child Within.*

To start, let's begin to look at 15 different feelings.

Unconditional Love ⎫
Bliss │
Joy │
Compassion and Empathy │
Enthusiasm │
Contentment ⎫ │
Fear │ │
Hurt │ │ Real Self
Sadness │ │
Shame and Guilt │ │
Anger ⎬ Co-dependent Self │
Confusion │ │
Emptiness │ │
Numbness ⎭ ⎭

These are arranged from the joyful ones at the top
to the more painful ones at the bottom half of the chart.

These feelings are also arranged to show that when we live
our life mostly from our false or co-dependent self, the result is that
most of the feelings that we feel are painful ones.
But when we expand into our Child Within, our Real Self,
we can now feel the *entire* spectrum of feelings
that are available to us as part of our crucial inner life.

**In addition to feeling the painful ones,
we can now feel joyful feelings.**

Notice that I do not use the terms "positive" or "negative"
to describe feelings. This is because labeling a painful feeling
as "negative" may imply that we should not have it,
or that we should somehow stuff it or negate it.

Quite the contrary!

As we heal, we learn that it is useful to **go into** these
painful feelings and to experience them as fully as we can.

Consider the following exercise. Look at the list of feelings above
and contemplate one feeling at a time.
Think about what percentage of your time over the past few months
you have spent feeling that feeling. If you are not sure,
make a guess.
Then write that percentage just to the left of the specific feeling.
If you don't come up with a number,
write a question mark or *"don't know."*

After you have done a part or all of that exercise,
if you have a few more minutes, reflect on how it was for you
to do that exercise. What was that like in your inner life?
Write your reflections in the space below or in your journal or diary.

Once we *get* a feeling, how can we handle it?
Below is a flow list to consider using
when *any* feeling comes up for us. I call it —

Using Feelings To Heal And Grow

1. *Recognize* that I am **feeling** *something*
2. *Feel* the feeling, e.g. *be* angry, or sad,
   or whatever the feeling may be
3. *Name* the feeling or the feelings, if more than one
4. Feel it **some more**
5. *Express it* in a **healthy** way
6. *Get it all out*, appropriately and safely
7. *Use it* constructively
8. *Stay* with it *or let go* of it, whichever you choose.

Would your Child Within be interested in seeing how it feels
to do that? If so, let your Child try the following.
The **next time** you feel a **feeling** or several feelings
coming up inside you, take some time for yourself
and go into that feeling or those feelings.
As you go into the feeling, follow those eight steps experientially.
If you wish, you could make some notes next to each step,
that correspond with each of these steps
regarding your experience. In these notes write
anything, whatever comes up for you. You can write about
either joyful or painful feelings. If you have any
questions about any of this, talk to a safe person,
including your therapy group or therapist.

62

Would you want to try doing this exercise from
the previous page more than once? If so, just insert
a blank paper over the bottom of this page and write
your reflections on your additional feeling experiences.
As we heal our Child Within, we can learn
several more important principles about feelings.

More Principles About Feeling

Fully experiencing our **feelings** helps us heal
our Child Within and we grow. It does this
by several mechanisms or actions —

It • Heightens our awareness of the type and intensity of our
  feelings.
  • Helps in connecting with close or intimate others.
  • Prevents build-up of resentment and depression.
  • Facilitates working through an upset or conflict.
  • " personal growth.
  • " growth in relationship.
  • " our realizing Serenity.

Reviewing the above, are there any of these
actions that you would like to happen in your life?
Place a check mark next to each one that you would like to happen.

Another principle is not to create any suffering
in our day-to-day life that we do not need.
I call this "unnecessary suffering," or "unnecessary pain."

For example, *healthy grieving* is necessary suffering.
But worrying ourself sick about something over which
we are powerless, or which is not *worth* our getting sick over,
may be unnecessary pain or suffering. So we gradually learn
that we *do not need to create* unnecessary suffering for ourselves.
This is distinctly different from numbing out.
I discuss this further in *Wisdom to Know the Difference.*

We can also observe any ways that we may *defend*
against the feelings. In addition to the classic
ego defenses (i.e., the defenses of the false self), we may also
block experiencing our feelings through addictions, compulsions
or other unhealthy attachments. We can call
any and all of these ways "medicating our feelings."

We can watch for **numbness**, which may mean
that we are avoiding the power of experiencing our feelings
by the defense of substituting one feeling for another —
in this case we can call it "numbing out."
Remember that numbness or shock, if transient
for an appropriate time, can be helpful in certain situations,
such as at the beginning of healthy grieving.

Sometimes one feeling substitutes automatically
for another, such that our original and pure feeling
is clouded over or even taken over by another.
This phenomenon is called **binding**.
One of the most common binders is **shame**.
Others are **anger, fear, confusion** and **guilt,** and
I just described **numbness** above.

(See also page 179 for a description of age regression,
which often has binding as a dynamic.)

Have you noticed the binding of any of your feelings
by any of these above feelings or by any other feelings?
As you go about your day-to-day life now,
would you be interested in observing and feeling
these feelings to such an extent that you begin
to notice which feelings come up first, and are thus
more original or pure, and which feelings may come in to bind them?
We can call these more original or pure feelings **primary** feelings
and the ones that come in and bind them **secondary** feelings, or
binders. As you observe and experience your feelings in this way,
feel free to write about some of these in the space below.

Would you like to take a break now?

A major way to know that we are healing our Child Within
is when we are becoming progressively more aware of our inner life,
which includes our feelings.

Keeping a Feelings Chart

Each time that we have a feeling, it may be useful
to us in some way, and thus be a primary feeling,
or it may just be bothersome and have less or even
no usefulness to us (and be a primary **or** secondary feeling).
In the latter case, we may *amplify* any feeling beyond
any practical usefulness, or we may create a perhaps
unnecessary feeling, as in the case of binding described above.
If our feelings can be so useful to us, as I have
described throughout this book and summarized in
this chapter (see especially page 63), then how can we
begin to recognize them, handle them and use them
in healing our Child Within?

One possible way is to keep a feelings chart
wherein we begin to "tune in" to a particular feeling
and give it a name. We can then briefly describe
the **situation** we are experiencing around that feeling.
Going further, we can ask ourself,
"What **needs** might this feeling be reflecting to me right now?"
and then write that down on the chart.

Finally, we can consider and reflect upon how this feeling is
or has been **useful** to us, and write some reflections about that.
Such a feelings chart is shown on the next two pages.
You may want to make some *extra copies* of it for future use.

As you experience, name, write about and reflect upon your feelings
as they come up for you, there are some ways
to strengthen your healing.
These ways include **sharing** your feeling experiences
with safe people, including your —

- Best friend
- Spouse
- Therapy group
- Therapist or counselor
- Sponsor
- _____
  (Fill in the blank)

Chart 9.1. Feelings Chart

Name of Feeling	Associated Situation And Experience

Feelings Chart (continued)

Associated Needs	Usefulness

As you share with one or more of these people, you have several choices regarding what you would like in response from them:

— Just to **listen** to you
— **Support** you
— Their **feedback**
— Their **response**
— Something you'd like *them* to **change**
— Or **something else** (you name it)

Since we can't read one another's minds,
we have to ask the other(s) specifically for what we want.

Another aid in using this feelings chart is to review some of
the **causes** of or **associations** with painful and joyful feelings.
We may feel painful feelings, such as emptiness,
fear, sadness, hurt, shame, guilt, anger, confusion and numbness
— either alone or in the combination — in **various situations**.
I list some of these situations below.

Some Associations with Painful Feelings

Not eating (I'm hungry). Or eating junk food.
Not sleeping, resting or recreating.
Using caffeine, nicotine, alcohol or other drugs.
Any drug withdrawal.
Loss, whether real or threatened.
Ungrieved loss or hurt.
Abandonment or rejection.
Not getting my needs met.
Conflict.
Being afraid (tends to aggravate, mask, or bind other feelings).

Have you noticed or experienced any of these associations
with any of your painful feelings?

For example . . .

If I'm hungry, I may feel some emptiness, guilt, shame, fear or
confusion. Or if I've just been abandoned, I may feel fear, hurt,
shame, guilt, anger or any other painful feeling. And if I've just
had a loss, I could feel *any* painful feeling. And each
of these feelings that we have, when we have them, would be
completely appropriate in association with the situation.

As we learn more about our feelings, we discover
that each feeling that we have is real.

It is absolutely **real**.

We **cannot** have a false or unreal feeling.

And **no one** can tell us which feeling to have.

Whatever feeling we have in each moment
is absolutely **true** for us. So,

We can have no right or wrong feelings.

There are only feelings that come up for us,
which I call primary feelings,
and those that we may somehow create around or over
them, which I call secondary feelings.

Both primary and secondary feelings are real and valid.
Differentiating the two is useful to help us work
through conflict and to heal our Child Within.

For example, we may feel angry around
a certain conflict, while underneath that anger
are bubbling fear and hurt. If all we feel
and work with is the anger, we may miss
the opportunity of healing ourselves around the conflict completely
because we have not experienced and worked through
the more primary feelings of fear and hurt.

Becoming aware of which feeling is primary and
which is secondary *does not negate* the secondary,
since it *is absolutely real* too.
Rather, this awareness helps us to discover
feelings that are often hidden and thus not
experienced and processed fully, so that
we are now able to heal that particular conflict
and thus help heal our Child Within.

Group therapy and **individual** therapy are usually excellent places
to work on and learn how to use these aspects of our feelings
in a healthy way.

Finally, we can review some of the causes of
or associations with joyful feelings, such as
contentment, enthusiasm, compassion, empathy,
joy, bliss and unconditional love.

Some Associations with Joyful Feelings

Getting my needs met.
Completing my griefwork and unfinished business.
Resolving conflict.
Healthy altered states of consciousness.
Meditation, prayer and other spiritual practices.
Feeling fulfilled.
Feeling loved.
Feeling infatuated (also called *limerance*).
Loving, giving love, or choosing love.
Letting go of fear.

Since these latter four are so difficult for many of us adult children
to deal with, I address them further in Chapters 26 and 27, and
in the books
Spirituality in Recovery and *Wisdom to Know the Difference.*

Did you have any reactions from any of the material in this chapter?

Use the space below to write and reflect upon
any of your feelings, thoughts or other reactions.

Time for a break?

10

Feeling Some More

As we go inside ourselves to our powerful inner life,
we become progressively more aware of
many of its aspects, dimensions and uses.

One big part of our inner life is our feelings.
To heal our Child Within, we become aware of our feelings.
We can begin to practice handling those feelings
using an approach like the one on page 62,
called "Using Feelings To Heal And Grow."
But if we choose to share and to communicate these feelings,
how do we decide *with whom* to share and communicate?

With whom might it be **safe** and **appropriate**
to share or communicate these feelings?
To assist in making such a decision,
I include Table 8 from page 81 of *HCW*.
This table shows at least four possibilities or choices
that we may have regarding when to
and when not to share our feelings.

Early Recovery

Early in recovery we may be closed to our feelings,
as represented in level 1 in the table (Closed).
Here we are neither aware of our feelings nor are we able
to use them constructively in our life.
And so while we may have superficial talk with many people,
we are not able to experience our feelings and to grow from them.
But just *recognizing* and being *aware* that this is what
we are doing is a start in our healing process.

Beginning to Explore our Feelings

As we begin to discover and to *feel* our feelings,
we may be *appropriately* guarded in sharing them.
They may come out disguised as ideas and opinions.
Since we may not yet be facile and skilled in experiencing
and using our feelings, we may not be able
to grow from them as fully as we will later.
And so to work through this level 2 we can take a risk
and begin to **practice** sharing our feelings with safe people —
such as our therapy group, therapist or best friend,
then asking them for feedback.

Would your Child Within be interested in coming out a bit
and trying an exercise in feelings? When a feeling
comes up for you, use the space below, or another space,
to write about it and to describe it.

Table 10.1. Levels of Awareness and Communication of Feelings, With
Guidelines for Sharing (modified from Dreitlein, 1984)

Our Feeling Condition	Communication	Self-Disclosure	Inter-personal Interaction and Ability To Grow	People With Whom To Share Our Feelings	
				Who Are Not Appropriate	Who Are Appropriate
1. Closed	Superficial conversation, reporting of facts	None Obvious facts	None	Selected people	Most people
2. Beginning to explore	Ideas and opinions to please others	Guarded Accidental	Little	People who do not listen	People who listen
3. Exploring and expressing	Genuine Gut level	Willingness Openness	Much	People who betray or reject us	People who are safe and supportive
4. Open, Expressing Observing	Optimal	Complete when life enhancing	Most	People who betray us or reject us	People who are safe and supportive

After you have described it, find a **safe** person or safe people
to share it with. You can tell them that for this exercise, all the
feedback that you want is *what they see* and what they *hear.*
After you have completed that, you might tell the person
what it was like for you to share the feeling and to get more
    feedback.
If you'd like, write what doing all of the above was like for you.

Exploring and Expressing our Feelings

Here we continue to risk and share our feelings
with safe people. Since we are becoming progressively more
aware of them, our feelings are now more genuine or "gut level,"
and we are more willing and open with them.
Here, we have much opportunity to experience and grow.

Try repeating the above exercise using another feeling,
this time risking some more and sharing with a **safe** person
from perhaps a deeper place in your inner life.

Open — Expressing and Observing our Feelings

At this level we become more comfortable and able
to trust our Child Within and that of others.
We now selectively share our feelings appropriately
with safe people. And as this kind of sharing continues and matures,
we can begin to *observe* our feelings. And as we do so,
we discover an empowering and healing principle —
we are not our feelings. While they are helpful
and even crucial to our aliveness and ability to know
and enjoy ourselves and others, we can at the same time
simply *observe* our feelings. Here we are at harmony
with our feelings. They no longer overtake us
or rule us. We are not their victim.

Can you think of any ways to experience this level
of being aware of, using and observing? Write these somewhere.
You might ask safe others, such as those in your therapy group
or your therapist, to discuss this question with you.

The Big Four Feelings in Healing:
Anger, Shame, Fear And Joy

I call these the "big four" feelings in healing
because they are some of the most difficult with which to deal.

Anger

Getting angry when it is appropriate is healing because it helps
us to:

- Discover **what happened** and what is happening
  to us and with us
- **Set limits** when appropriate
- **Grieve** our hurts and losses
- Get our **needs** met
- Get things off our chest
- Be **assertive**
- Influence or change others (when possible)
- Discover what is **underneath** our anger
- Realize and experience **serenity** and
- Understand and accept other people's anger,
  without decompensating ourself.

It may be helpful now to read the pages
in **HCW** on getting angry (pages 99-101).

When we get angry, what choices do we have?
Before looking at the next list, pause and reflect a minute
on this question. Write any choices you may know of.

Some choices in handling anger may include —
  1. Stuff it and experience mostly numbness.
  2. Hold it in, in the form of a resentment
     until it becomes unbearable.
  3. Unable to let it out, get physically or emotionally sick.
  4. Medicate the pain with a person, place, thing, behavior
     or experience, such as alcohol, drugs, eating, sex, work, etc. or
  5. Express the anger — and other feelings —
     and work through it with safe people.

Which of these were you taught to use when you got angry?
Which were modeled for you? Make an "X" mark
and any notes you like next to the ones that
you were taught or had modeled growing up.
Which of these do you use now? Make a "check" mark by these.

When we find one or more safe people, such as in our therapy
group or elsewhere, there are several experiential techniques or
vehicles that we can use to work through that anger.

Some Experiential Techniques to Assist in Working Through Anger

- *Telling our story,* including the anger (see Chapter 21).

- *Naming what happened,* including how we were mistreated or hurt, and expressing our anger and other feelings around it.

- *Expressing* our anger *directly to the person* with whom we are angry. The safer the person, the more likely will we be able to resolve our anger. I advise against using this method with an unsafe person until you have spent some time weighing the advantages and disadvantages of doing so. Discuss these with your therapy group, therapist, best friend or similar safe person. I describe anger in detail in *Wisdom to Know the Difference* and in a talk on anger in volume 2 of my audiotapes on core recovery issues.

- *Being assertive* — This is useful when combined with any of the other techniques, depending on the details behind the anger. Learning to be assertive when appropriate is an important part of healing our Child Within. It is the Child itself — our True Self — that is assertive. Being assertive means that we get what we want or need without hurting ourself or another person. We can **practice** being assertive with safe people. Then later we can be assertive with anyone, depending on the situation and on the appropriateness of being assertive. There are courses on assertiveness training offered in many communities through local educational facilities. I discuss being assertive in my book on Boundaries And Limits.

- Using *psychodrama techniques,* such as role play, family sculpture or other gestalt techniques. These are best done in group therapy and can be done in limited form in individual therapy.

- Doing *anger bat* work — this is also best done in group therapy or individual therapy, using a safe anger bat or "bataka," supervised by a therapist skilled in using this kind of healing technique. Anger bat work can be used constructively in combination with many of the other methods.

- Writing an *unmailed letter* (see page 161)

- Writing in our *diary* or *journal*

- Using *active imagination* (see page 156)

- *Grieving* — Anger is a healthy part of the grieving process, which I describe in Chapter 22 of this book and in *HCW.*

You may think of other techniques to assist you
in working through anger,
including working the Twelve Steps.

On the last two pages of this chapter are spaces to work out a
    specific plan to handle anger or resentment as it comes up in
    your healing process. As you work out your plan, consider the
    following . . .

What or whom may you be angry at or about?

What do you want to happen regarding the situation
and about your anger or resentment?

Which of the above methods or techniques might you use
to help heal or get rid of your anger or resentment?

Finally, after you have done your anger work,
what are the results?

We can use many of the experiential techniques described in this
section and throughout this book, including Chapters 17 and 18,
to help heal **fear** and **shame**
and to help us let go into experiencing **joy**.

Especially helpful in healing **shame** is
telling our story about our shame with safe people.
Group therapy is a constructive setting to do such healing,
as is individual therapy, and a talk with a best friend.
Attending Twelve Step meetings and working the Steps
are also effective methods for healing shame.

These and other techniques are also helpful in healing **fear**.

Another technique when fear is bothering us is to write at the top
left of a blank page *What could happen?* and draw a vertical line
about 1/3 way from the left. To its right, write *How Would I Handle
It?* Next to each event that could happen as a result of what I am
afraid of, which I've just written under *What could Happen?,* I then
write to its right *How I would Handle it.*

Spiritual practices are especially helpful with fear as well.

In the space below, list the major feelings that you
have the most difficulty with in recognizing, experiencing,
handling and letting go of. To the right of each,
write a plan that you can use to assist you in your healing.

Chart 10.1. Handling My Anger

What or Whom am I Angry at or Resentful About?	What I Want to Happen Regarding the Situation and My Anger/Resentment

Chart 10.1. Handling My Anger

Possibilities and/or Plan and Techniques to Help Heal my Anger/Resentment	What Happened After or Results

Notes

11

Stress In My Life

Stress can be useful or destructive.

A goal in healing our Child Within is to make the stress
in our life as useful as possible for our well-being
and growth without creating any unnecessary stress.

Growing up in a troubled or unhealthy family
may have left us with two temporary handicaps:

- We were either *not taught* how to handle
  stress in a healthy way and/or we were
  taught unhealthy ways to handle it, and

- We *accumulated* a lot of unhandled
  stress, and because we never had a chance to work through
  its associated conflict, this *continues* to cripple us emotionally.

A reason that the Child went into hiding
was that it sensed overwhelming stress
and it didn't know how to handle it.

It didn't feel safe.

For the Child Within to come out of hiding,
it needs to feel safe.

In healing our Child Within, we learn
- To make as safe an environment for ourselves as we can.
- We heal with safe people.
- We get our needs met.
- We are attentive to and experience our vital inner life.

To help prevent our being over stressed (distressed) we can
- Exercise physically, in moderation.
- Eat healthy food.
- Work through our conflicts constructively.
- And begin daily spiritual practices, such as meditation,
  prayer or reading spiritual literature.

And as we do these little by little
— beginning to take care of and nurture
our Child, progressively, more and more —
we can take a look back at our past
and at how we might have been distressed growing up.

In this chapter I reproduce some parts of Chapter 7 on
The Role of Stress: the Post-Traumatic Stress Disorder from *HCW*.
I will follow this reading material with some healing exercises.

The post-traumatic stress disorder (PTSD) is a condition that may so affect someone that not only is the Child Within stifled and stunted, but the person often becomes overtly ill from repeated stress and its extreme traumas. The PTSD interacts with the dynamics of co-dependence to such an extent that these two conditions often overlap. What Kritsberg (1986) describes as "chronic shock" among children of alcoholics can be equated to PTSD.

PTSD may occur across a spectrum of manifestations, from fear or anxiety, or depression, to easy irritability, to impulsive or even explosive behavior. To determine whether PTSD is present, the DSM III suggests that the following four conditions be present.

1. Recognizable Stressor

The first is the history of the ongoing presence of a recognizable *stressor*. Some examples and degress of stressors are shown in the DSM III and are reproduced in a modified form in Table 11.1 below. While there are countless other examples, I have italicized several of the stressors found among troubled or dysfunctional families.

Table 11.1. Severity Rating of Psychosocial Stressors
(from DSM III)

Code Term	Adult Examples	Child/Adolescent Examples
1. None	No apparent psychological stressor	No apparent psychological stressor
2. Minimal	Minor violation of the law; small bank loan	Vacation with family
3. Mild	Argument with neighbor; change in work hours	Change in school teacher; new school year
4. Moderate	New career; death of close friend; pregnancy	*Chronic parental fighting; change to new school; illness of close relative;* sibling birth
5. Severe	Serious *illness in self or family;* major financial loss; marital *separation;* birth of child	Death of peer; *divorce* of parents; arrest; hospitalization; *persistent and harsh parental discipline*
6. Extreme	*Death* of close relative; *divorce*	*Death* of parent or sibling; *repeated physical/sexual abuse*
7. Catastrophic	Concentration camp experience; devastating natural disaster	*Multiple family deaths*

Reflect on the section above under the
Child/Adolescent Examples,
and make a circle around or underline any stressors
that may have happened to you growing up.

If you are uncertain whether a particular stressor
may have happened to you, mark it anyway
and add a question mark next to it.

What we are doing in our continued healing here is to
give another name or names to what happened.

Doing so is part of our healing process.

To facilitate this part of the healing process
it is helpful to write in your own handwriting
what happened. The space on the next page
is for organizing this information.

Chart 11.1. Stressors From My Past

	Adulthood	Childhood and Adolescence
Stressors Marked from Table 11.1		
Uncertain Questionable Stressors		
From My Past Other Stressors not listed in Table 11.1		

Take your time in writing these events.
Once you have written in and named
any stressful events or happenings
from your childhood or your adolescence,
begin to reflect back on your **adult** life.
What stressful events have happened
to you since you were an adult?
For some examples, review the list of adult examples
listed in Table 11.1 (on page 83).

A stressful event could be any moderate life event
or major event that upset you in any way
or was hard or difficult for you in any way.
It may also be any of the mistreatments that you have
experienced or remembered from working through
any of the other chapters.

As they come into your mind,
as you think of them, write any stressful events
or mistreatments that have happened to you as an adult
in the space under **Adulthood** on the previous page.

Take as much time as you need in writing these events.

Having completed these lists for now, if you would like to explore
further the effect of that stress on your life, of what happened to you,
refer back to Table 11.1 and look at the numbers next to the
examples. These numbers increase as the event becomes more
stressful. What number might you assign to each of the events on
your two written lists on page 84?

Look over each stressful event on your list on page 84
and assign an approximate number that corresponds
to its severity, using the numbers 1-7 under the Code Term
in Table 11.1. Then *average* all these numbers.
If the average is 4 or more, this could be a clue that you
might have some degree of PTSD present even today.

Write in your PTSD average here: _____ points

As a child, an adolescent and an adult,
how did you handle these stresses?

Did anyone teach you healthy ways to handle these?

Or were you taught the opposite?
Write about your experience.

**If we didn't get to handle these stresses
in a healthy way, they may be still affecting us
as adults. Is it possible that I may have
some degree of PTSD?**

From this short list of examples one can see that stressors are commonly found in families and environments that tend to stifle the True Self. However, to determine the presence of PTSD, the type of stressor must be outside the usual range of human experience. Examples of such stressors may include assault, rape, other sexual abuse, serious physical injury, torture, concentration camp experience, floods, earthquakes, military combat and the like. I believe, as do others (Cermak, 1985), that growing up or living in a seriously troubled or dysfunctional family or similar environment often brings about or is associated with PTSD. The PTSD is said to be more damaging and more difficult to treat if: (1) the traumas occur over a *prolonged* period of time, *e.g.,* longer than six months; and especially so if (2) the traumas are of *human origin*; and if (3) those around the affected person tend to *deny* the existence of the stressor or the stress. All three are present in an actively alcoholic family and in similar troubled families.

As you continue reading, make a note in the margin if you have had or *continue to have* any of the following.

Re-experiencing the Trauma

The second condition or manifestation is the re-experiencing of the trauma. This may be a history of recurrent and intrusive recollections of the trauma, recurrent bad dreams or nightmares, or sudden symptoms of re-experiencing the trauma, often with rapid heart rate, panic and sweating.

Psychic Numbing

An outstanding characteristic of the Child Within or True Self is that it feels and expresses feelings. The co-dependent or false self denies and covers up genuine feelings. This advanced condition, called psychic numbing, is characteristic of PTSD. It may be manifested by a constriction or absence of feeling and of expressing feelings, which often results in a sense of estrangement, withdrawal, isolation or alienation. Another manifestation may be a decreased interest in important life activities.

Describing psychic numbing, Cermak (1986) writes, "During moments of extreme stress, combat soldiers are often called upon to act regardless of how they are feeling. Their survival depends upon their ability to suspend feelings in favor of taking steps to ensure their safety. Unfortunately, the resulting "split" between one's self and one's experience does not heal easily. It does not gradually disappear with the passage of time. Until an active process of healing takes place, the individual continues to experience a *constriction of feelings, a decreased ability to recognize which feelings* are present and a persistent

sense of being cut off from one's surroundings (depersonalization).
These add up to a condition known as *psychic numbing."*

Other Symptoms

Another symptom of PTSD may be *hyperalertness* or *hypervigilance.*
The person is so fearful about continued stress, that he or she is
constantly on the alert for any and all potential similar stressors or
dangers, and how to avoid them. Yet another symptom is *survivor guilt,*
i.e., guilt felt after escaping or avoiding some of the trauma when
others are still in the trauma. While survivor guilt is said to lead to the
feeling that the survivor has betrayed or abandoned others, and often
then to chronic depression, I believe that several other factors lead to
chronic depression, primarily the stifling of the Child Within. Still
another manifestation of PTSD may be inappropriate use of psychoactive drugs, especially sedatives, and chemical dependence.

Another symptom may be *avoiding activities associated* with the
trauma. A final symptom, not listed in DSM III, is *multiple personalities.*
People with multiple personalities often come from highly troubled,
stressed or dysfunctional families. Perhaps multiple personalities are
often offshoots of the false or co-dependent self, driven in part, by the
energies of the True Self to express itself.

Cermak (1985) suggests that the dynamics of the condition known
as "adult child of alcoholic," "CoA syndrome," or other similar terms
are a combination of *PTSD* and *co-dependence.* From my experience
treating ACoAs and following them in their recovery, as well as treating
adult children from *other* troubled or dysfunctional families, I believe
that PTSD and co-dependence are likely to be a part of many troubled
or dysfunctional families. I further believe that PTSD is but an extreme
extension of the broad condition that results from stifling the True Self
in any form. When we are not allowed to remember, to express our
feelings and to grieve or mourn our losses or traumas, whether real or
threatened, through the free expression of our Child Within, we become ill. Thus we can consider viewing a spectrum of unresolved
grieving as beginning with mild symptoms or signs of grief to co-
dependence to PTSD. A common thread in this spectrum is the blocked
expression of our True Self.

Treatment of PTSD consists of long-term group therapy with others
who suffer from the condition and usually as needed shorter term
individual counseling. Many of the treatment principles for healing our
Child Within are helpful in treating PTSD.

While you might need a trained professional therapist to assist you in self-diagnosing PTSD, by now you might have some sense of whether you may have had and/or continue to have any of these manifestations of PTSD. Below is a checklist for you to summarize your experiences.

Chart 11.2. PTSD Checklist

Manifestation of PTSD	In My Past?	Still Have It?	Any Description Of Or Comments About The Event Or Experience
Stressful Life Events			
Score = Average 4 or more			
Recurrent Bad Memories			
Recurrent Scary Dreams			
Panic Attacks			
Psychic Numbing			
Hyperalertness			
Survivor Guilt			
Avoiding Associ- ated Activities			

Here write a **YES** or a **NO** to indicate presence or absence of symptom from the left column

Some *other manifestations* of *chronic distress* and PTSD
may include:
- "Walking on eggs" (or "eggshells") which is a feeling
  of chronic fear and inability to be real and
  spontaneous, especially when around unsafe people
- Phobias
- Nameless fears or "free floating" anxiety
- Fear of abandonment
- Fear of others' anger or rejection
- Fear of the unknown
- Recurring fatigue
- Recurring illness
- Multiple personality
- Fear of being exposed or shamed

The way to heal any degree of PTSD
is to heal our Child Within.

Thus the methods described in this workbook
and in *HCW* for healing our Child Within are useful
for helping to heal any degree of PTSD that we may have.

If you are slowly working through this book, chapter by chapter,
you are helping to heal any PTSD that you may have.

In the space below and on the next page,
write any memories, reactions or experiences
that have come up for you
while you were reading or working through this chapter.

Notes

12

What Is A Healthy Family?

For a number of reasons, most people who grew up
in a troubled, unhealthy or dysfunctional family
think the opposite about that family.
They think their family was okay, normal, functional.

As we begin and progress in our recovery,
we may come to see that our family was not okay
or that parts of it were not okay.
For us, our family may have even been unhealthy.
It may have wounded our True Self, our Child Within.

We can begin to look at family functioning
by drawing a horizontal line representing
the spectrum or range of its possible functioning.
At the far right is the ideal healthy family,
where the psychological and spiritual
well-being and growth of each member is met.

And at the far left is the least healthy
family, the most dysfunctional.

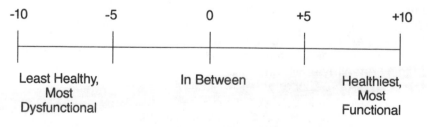

Figure 12.1. Family Functioning

Virginia Satir, who back in 1951 was perhaps the first
family therapist, estimated that about 95% of families in
this country were troubled, unhealthy or dysfunctional in some way.

As I have worked with adult children in their healing process
and as I have surveyed colleagues, friends and others,
I have come to agree with her estimate of 95%.

I also have a strong clinical impression that if we were to draw
a bell-shaped curve of a statistically normal distribution
over this range or spectrum, that it might look something like this.

Figure 12.2. Family Functioning Distribution

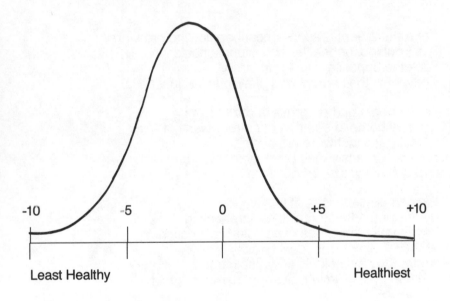

How growing up in an unhealthy family
affects the child is by wounding its
True Self, its Child Within.
It forces its True Self to go into hiding.
And what emerges to help it survive
in this unhealthy environment is
the false or co-dependent self.
The child, as it grows into an adult,
then becomes addicted or unhealthily attached
to its false or co-dependent self.

Let's examine two words that are
commonly used in recovery and elsewhere:
Normal and *Functional.*

Normal is most accurately a statistical term,
referring to what is most common, standard or usual.
Even though some people have used it to imply healthy,
it does not mean healthy.

So in speaking of **families,** to use the word normal
would actually mean "statistically most common,"
which is troubled, unhealthy or dysfunctional.
Rather than use the word normal,
when I really mean *healthy,*
I prefer to go ahead and say **healthy.**

Functional implies that something is working.
So for a family we can ask, "Is it working?"
To me, working or functioning optimally
means that the family is supporting
the psychological and spiritual well-being
and growth of each of its members.
That is my basic definition of a functional, healthy family.

But we can use "functional" in another way,
a way that many adult children may use it or have used it
about their own family at one time or another.
In doing so, they may include the following facts:

"I always . . . had a roof over my head
            . . . had food on the table
            . . . had a school to attend, and
            . . . got presents on special occasions."
"And since I also was not physically
or sexually abused, my conclusion
may be that my family was not dysfunctional."

Does this make sense?

Is there anything missing in this kind of reasoning?
If you think that there is, write what you
sense is missing in the space below.

In my sense, there is a lot missing in this reasoning.

Important things like:

- needs
- feelings
- grieving
- communication
- intimacy and
- our Child Within

When talking in this way about families, I prefer to use the words *healthy or unhealthy.*

To review: A **healthy family** is basically one that *supports the psychological and spiritual well-being and growth of each of its members.*

An unhealthy family **doesn't.**

So while being helpful, being materially well off does not make a healthy family.

What was your family of origin like?

If you have worked the prior chapters, you probably have an accurate idea by now.

Would you be interested in doing an exercise that might give you some more insight into how healthy your own family of origin might have been?

If so, on the next pages read over the 36 characteristics of a healthy and an unhealthy family. Think about *where* on this spectrum, reproduced at the top of each page, you would estimate that your own family of origin was when you were a child. Mark an "X" on the page about where on the spectrum you estimate that your family was for each of the 36 characteristics.

Before doing this exercise fully, read the cautions on the next page.

After completing this exercise, you have at least two choices:

1. By a kind of "eyeball" technique, make a rough impression of where on the spectrum your family was.
   Or
2. By assigning a number (-10 through 10) to *each of the 36 items,* add up all the numbers and divide that total by 36. That will provide an *approximate* number describing your impression of how healthy your family was. (Note: -5 plus + 1 = -4; -3 plus -2 = -5. Example: for a total of -54, dividing by 36 would give the answer -1.5.)

Here are some **cautions** in using this exercise.

Depending on where you are in your own personal recovery, your estimation of where your family was on each item may vary somewhat. That variation may be enough to make a +1 into a -2 or vice versa.

So don't blame yourself or beat yourself up if the overall figure comes out to be something like a +1 or +2 and you are a confused or unhappy person. You might have overestimated your family's health or you might have had a lot of losses, hurts and trauma *since* you left your family of origin. Or you might have other issues.

This kind of situation is where it can be helpful to talk to a professional therapist who has training in adult child recovery work and knows family dynamics.

Also in doing this exercise, don't estimate where your family of origin is now. The estimate in this exercise is of where it was *when* **you** *were growing up as a child.*

Finally, don't compare your family's score with other peoples' family score, and don't reason that if your family score was a -1 or a -2 — or even a +5 — that you don't have any recovery work to do.

Also, you don't have to change your experiences if other family members report that they had a different experience.

Chart 12.1. My Family Of Origin

```
-10            -5              0            +5            +10
 |─────────────┼──────────────┼─────────────┼─────────────|
```

Least Healthy,   In Between   Healthiest,
    Most   Most
Dysfunctional   Functional

Unhealthy Family	Healthy Family
Not working: psycho-spiritual well-being and growth of each member not supported.	Working: psycho-spiritual well-being and growth of each member supported.
Not allowed. Co-dependent, false self, negative ego predominates.	Real Self of each accepted and nurtured.
Not accepted or supported.	Needs of each accepted and supported.
Not accepted or expressed.	Feelings accepted and expressed.
Closed. Denial, including of dysfunction. Secrets common. No listening. Facade of "normality."	Communication open. Listening.
Intimacy vacuums. Closeness at times.	Intimacy experienced.
Compulsions, addictions and illness in most.	Healthy people generally.
Most are martyr or victim.	Members aware and responsible.
Discouraged, not supported.	Grieving of loss and hurt supported.
Shame-based. Judgmental. Esteem discouraged.	Healthy self-esteem encouraged and supported.
Unspoken and vague. Rigid, anti-growth, anti-life.	Rules clear and explicit, yet flexible when appropriate.
Vague, rigid and fused (enmeshed) or too loose triangles.	Boundaries clear and flexible.
Rigid to chaotic.	Attitudes and beliefs healthy and open
Rigid, from past only.	Traditions present and flexible.
Criticism, manipulation and need to control.	Constructive feedback.
Not free. Conformity demanded, often subtle.	Freedom, and members free to be unique and individual.
Suspicious and jealous.	Trusting and loving.
Unpleasant.	Atmosphere pleasant.

My Family Of Origin

-10	-5	0	+5	+10

Least Healthy,
Most
Dysfunctional

In Between

Healthiest,
Most
Functional

Unhealthy Family	**Healthy Family**
Mistreating. Neglecting.	Fair and democratic.
Often attacking and blaming.	Members introspect appropriately.
Inconsistent. Arbitrary. Unpredictable.	Continuity. Consistency.
Absent to unhealthy.	Recreation, play and humor healthy.
Some families rigid. Chaotic at times. Quiet and functional at times. Range across a spectrum of dysfunction.	Healthy functioning and support.
Unbalanced.	Pursuing and distancing balanced.
Not so. Intrusive.	Privacy respected and supported.
Rigid. Dictated by families' needs.	Roles individualized.
Scarcity principle.	Abundance principle.
Absent or conditional.	Love in abundance.
Unavailable, inappropriate, inconsistent.	Focused attention appropriate (physical, mental, emotional, spiritual).
Discouraged or disallowed.	Mistakes allowed.
Discouraged or disallowed.	Individuality and uniqueness supported.
Absent to minimal.	Sense of belonging.
Fragmented.	Feeling of wholeness.
Often constant or threat of.	Conflict occasional to frequent.
Indirect and unresolved.	Conflict faced directly and resolved.
Potential for recovery.	Personal power through awareness and responsibility.

All that this exercise *is* —
is to begin giving you some guidelines
regarding how healthy or unhealthy
your family of origin was when you
were growing up as a child and an adolescent.

If you want to use this method for evaluating
your *current* family, wherein you might be a parent, for example,
you are free to do that. Just remember
that doing so is a completely separate exercise.

I repeat: If you have any difficulties with this or any exercise or
concept in this book, consult a professional therapist with training in
working with the recovery of adult children
of troubled, unhealthy or dysfunctional families.

How was it for you to do (or even just to read over) that exercise?
If you choose, write your answer in the space below.
Feel free to write whatever comes up for you.

These 36 traits of healthy and unhealthy families are from my own clinical
impressions and experiences, and some are also borrowed or modified
from Curran's *Traits of a Healthy Family*, Wegscheider-Cruse's *Choicemaking*
and Cermak's *A Time to Heal*.

13

Secrets

Were there any secrets in your family?

Do you remember any?

A secret is • Anything we are told not to tell,
and • Anything important that people may have kept from us.

There are two kinds of secrets: Healthy and Toxic.
Keeping a toxic secret can be damaging to us.
It may lower our self-esteem, increase our guilt,
block our ability to grieve our losses and hurts
and weaken our immune system.
In short, it may block our serenity.

A **healthy** secret is a **confidence.**
If we keep that secret
and we do not tell it,
we will not be harmed,
and neither will anyone else.

By contrast, if we keep a **toxic** secret,
or if someone keeps an important secret from *us,*
which is also toxic, we may be harmed.

The point is not that we have to go out now and tell all our secrets or even someone else's secret.

What tends to be most healing for us is that —

A. we come to know any important secrets that may have been kept from us, and that

B. we tell to a *safe person* any toxic secret that may be damaging us.

Below are some examples of each category of secrets.

Toxic Secrets — Type 1 —

Secrets Kept from Children and Others

- A parent or relative has a life-threatening illness (e.g., alcoholism, drug dependence, cancer, etc.).

- A parent or relative has an embarrassing condition or illness (e.g., compulsive gambling, sexual addiction, mental illness, loss of an important job or position, impotence, lack of sexual desire, was in a concentration camp or the like).

- A child was mistreated or hurt due to a problem in one or both of the parents and/or between them.

(As an example, a father and mother are both unable to handle their personal conflicts; their son is affected by the conflicts and in response he "acts out"; they blame him and send him away to boarding school.)

These are usually secrets not known by the child.
To *others* in the family, the information
may be • known, • unclear or only partly known or • unknown.

(As an example, Barbara, age 48, was the youngest of eight children in her troubled family. When Barbara was 16, her older sister told her that she, her older sister, was actually her mother, and that she had not seen the father after Barbara was born. In addition to a number of difficulties and issues in her life Barbara had much difficulty trusting people and had a lot of shame. She was so embarrassed and hurt by this information, that she kept it to herself for nearly 30 years until she got into counseling. When she told her secret to the members of her therapy group, she got validated, supported and affirmed for her feelings and difficulties all these years. Feeling that the therapy group was a safe place, she was able to progressively know and be her True Self, her Child Within. She thereby got free of most of the toxicity of this secret.)

Barbara's story illustrates a Type 1 toxic secret that, because she discovered it, became a Type 2 toxic secret.

Secrets That May Be Damaging Us

These are secrets that we may know fully,
partially, or that we may have even repressed.

Some examples of this kind of secret include —

- I was sexually mistreated or abused

- I was mistreated by violence

- I hurt or tried to hurt someone severely

- Someone hurt or tried to hurt me severely

- I did something that was really bad

Sometimes secrets can be so emotionally charged or threatening
to us or to others that we or they
shut them completely out of awareness (i.e., repress it).

So we may have secrets that we don't even know we have.
Or we may minimize a secret.

> For example, our father is gone a lot having affairs, but we say he
> deserves to leave, the way our mother nags him.

In healing our Child Within, we may **discover** secrets
that have been *kept from* that little Child (Type 1 toxic secrets)
and/or, as part of our healing, we may **tell** secrets (Type 1 or 2)
to safe people that have damaged that little Child.

While we are still learning about the psychology and physiology of
secrets, we are coming to see that **discovering** and/or **telling**
secrets to **safe people** may well:

- Increase our self-esteem

- Decrease our shame and guilt

- Allow us to grieve our ungrieved hurts

- Strengthen our body's immune system, and

- Increase our ability to love and be loved.

In discovering and telling secrets,
we can go only as far as we wish to go.

1. One choice is just to **remember** the secret.
2. Another is to **write** it down in a **safe** place,
   like in this book or in our journal or diary.
3. Still another is to **tell** a **safe** person.
4. And finally, we may choose to tell **more** than
   just one safe person, e.g. we may tell
   the members of our therapy group.

While doing so may feel scary,
and while there are no 100% guarantees,
discovering and telling these kinds of secrets
is usually healing.

If you remember a secret
and if you would like to try writing anything about it,
feel free to use the space below.

If writing it here or in your diary or journal
is too scary for you right now,
consider writing it on a piece of paper
that you can hide in a safe place.
You can even tear it up and throw it away
after you have written it.

If you can't think of a secret to write, you might consider writing
about the most shameful or horrible thing or things that you've
ever done.

How did it feel to write what you did?
If you choose, write your responses about how it felt,
and how it feels now, in the space below.

If you decide to tell any secret(s)
to a safe person, here are some guidelines.

Because they are ethically bound to keep
everything you tell them as confidential
(with the exception of your seriously threatening
taking your own life or someone else's)
a therapist may be the safest person to tell.

Perhaps the next safest would be a long-term therapy group
that is led by trained professionals.
And this may be more healing than telling only one person.

And the next safest, depending on the person,
might be a best friend, perhaps the one you chose in the
chapter on *Who Is Safe To Talk To?*

Whether you have any reservations or not
about doing any of these actions described
in this chapter, it may be helpful
to write about them in the space below.
Feel free to write about *whatever* comes up for you around
this **whole idea of secrets.**

When we tell a secret, we don't have
to tell all of it. We can tell only a part of it
and then check the safe person's response.
If it feels safe, we can tell them more, either now or later.
This process is what Gravitz and Bowden call
"Share-Check-Share."

Choose your safe person or group carefully. They should have
demonstrated being safe for you over a fair length of time.
If you decided to tell your secret(s) and actually
told all or a part, what did doing that feel like?
And having told one or more secrets, how do you feel now?

Finally, what ideas or plans might you have now
for what you do with the information in the secret?

If you have any questions about this, it might be helpful
to go over them with your safe person or safe people.

After you have told a secret or secrets, and you have completed
any healing work around it or around them, you might not need
to do anything more with it.

Some criteria for knowing you've completed your work might
include that the secret(s) and/or the feelings associated
with them *no longer nag* you or bother you.

Another criterion might be that you *stop repeating* the same
self-destructive or other-destructive behavior that was
a manifestation of the kept secret.

These kinds of secrets can be difficult to deal with.
If you have any doubts about them, you might wish to
re-read this chapter sometime. And talk to a safe person.

Notes

Notes

If working through any of this material in any part of this book gets to be too painful or confusing for you, I suggest that you contact a professional therapist for a consultation (see page 130), and that you slow down on your use of this material.

14

A Full Recovery Program

Part 1
. . . A Beginning

If I were a repair person and had a toolbox,
were I to know what was *wrong* with something,
I could reach into that toolbox
and find and select one or several
tools that would assist me in my repair.

It is both interesting and exciting
to be alive at this time in human evolution.
This is in large part because we now have available
to each of us an emerging technology
for self-healing that before now was not so readily available.
If I were to be bold and take a risk,
I would summarize this self-healing
in just four words:

Healing my Child Within

I can begin to outline some of this
self-healing art and technology
by briefly describing where a person
might be on a continuum of recovery.
This recovery continuum has three stages.

Let's start by recognizing "the problem,"
which really is not a problem,
but is rather a wounding, a woundedness,
a deep hurt that caused the Child to go into hiding.

To survive, the child turns the running
of its life over to its ego,
which then becomes its false, adapted or co-dependent self.
The false self is actually *incompetent* to run our life
with wholeness, sanity and health.
The person becomes fragmented
and remains so, in chronic pain.

So out of this fragmentation or lack of wholeness, and
depending upon the person's environment,
a physical or **mental illness** or **condition develops.**
Some people might call that a **"problem"** or a condition,
while others might call it just a **manifestation of the loss**
of their True Self, and still others would call it
a **search** for their True Self, their Child Within.

Could it be that all three are true?
— a condition, a manifestation and a search?

Stage Zero Recovery

When this problem, illness or condition is **active,**
I call it *Stage Zero* recovery.
Recovery has not yet started.

These active conditions could include such things as:

- Addictions
- Any physical illness

- Compulsions
- Any mental illness

- Unhealthy attachments
- Any other condition

These conditions might be acute or recurring or chronic.

Depending on their nature, these conditions
might heal spontaneously or require
specific intervention and/or linger on
for a long time, even for a lifetime.

Could it be that each of these conditions is
an unsuccessful attempt by the body and the mind to heal?

Stage One recovery includes whatever specific methods
or actions it might take to facilitate the healing
of that active illness or condition.
Using, then, that **specific full recovery program**
for that **specific active** illness or **condition,**
this early healing, or at the least the achievement
of a solid and stable **recovery,**
may take a few months to a few years,
depending on the nature of the chronic condition.

Once that Stage Zero condition is healed or stable,
it may be time — as we by now may have a choice —
to begin to heal our fragmented self,
to re-discover our True Self and to
heal our Child Within.
We can call this *Stage Two* recovery.
This stage can also be called Adult Child recovery,
and the central metaphor and healing for it
is healing the Child Within.

While clinical observation and research are still ongoing,
it appears that for most people
who have been through their own Stage One recovery,
if appropriate, this Stage Two recovery
takes about three to five additional years,
depending upon the severity and nature
of the person's woundedness and on
their commitment to and work within
their adult child specific full recovery program.

By several and varied ways, such as
self-psychology, humanistic and transpersonal psychology,
and the adult child and co-dependence movements,
we have discovered that the **goal** of this
stage of recovery *is* the Child Within.

From my observations and experience,
I believe that the Child Within, our True Self,
is also the **vehicle** by which we recover.
Inherent and inborn into its delicate
and powerful nature is the capability
and the energy to heal itself.

So it is its own "repair person."

But not only was it not taught exactly
how to repair itself, it was frequently
taught the opposite — how to fragment itself.

It has to re-learn, or learn anew,
how to heal itself.
This healing is a large part
of this mysterious adventure
that we call being human.

In this book, and in the other books
that I have written, and in some
of those other books in their reference pages,
are some ways, some tools, to heal.

Since I am my own repair person,
I can now look for a toolbox
into which I might reach to find
the right tools to help in my repair work.

Let's open our toolbox now
and take a look inside.
I've learned by now that I don't even have to be
mechanically inclined to look into a toolbox
and to examine its contents.

The *first tool* is to **find** and **recognize**
any **active Stage Zero** conditions
that I might have.

This finding and recognizing is useful
because any such active condition
can *distract* my time and energy from
healing my Child Within.
So what is distracting me from devoting my healing
time and energy to that little wounded Child within me?

On page 108 is a list of six categories of possible conditions
or distractions. Some of these are defined further on pages 45-46
in Chapter 6 on *What Happened?* (Family Tree).

There is no rush to find and recognize these conditions
that may exist in myself.
For many people it takes weeks, months
or even years to do so.

And when you have some ideas, some names
for these conditions or possible distractions,
and when you have some time, you might
consider writing those names on the next page.

These conditions could be any of a large number —
such as overworking, workaholism, an eating disorder,
drinking or using other drugs too much,
alcoholism or other drug dependence, overly
worrying about or trying to control others (co-dependence),
compulsive neatness or compulsive housecleaning,
sexual addiction, a debilitating physical problem
or illness, a mental illness or some other condition.

If you have any difficulty finding or recognizing
any distractions like these in your life,
you might consider talking to a helping professional
who has expertise in your specific area(s) of concern.

Stage One Recovery

A *second tool* for healing is to begin
and to continue a **Stage One recovery program**
corresponding to each Stage Zero condition you might have.
To assist in this undertaking, the above-mentioned
helping professional may also be helpful.

When you have a plan or even an idea
and when you have some time, write in an outline
of your recovery program in the space
next to the corresponding condition (on the next page).

I include some example conditions and plans on the next page.

Chart 14.1. Your Recovery Programs

Stage Zero Condition	Corresponding Stage One Recovery Program

— Example Conditions And Recovery Programs —

Stage Zero Condition	Corresponding Stage One Recovery Program
Eating disorder	1. Attend two Overeaters Anonymous meetings each week 2. Work the OA program with a sponsor 3. If I need more help, see a counselor
Alcoholism or other chemical dependence	1. Abstain from alcohol and drugs, one day at a time 2. Attend AA or Narcotics Anonymous meetings weekly 3. Work the Twelve Steps with a sponsor 4. Group therapy, CD - specific weekly, long term 5. Individual counseling as needed
Sexual addiction	1. Attend Sex and Love Addicts Anonymous, Sexaholics Anonymous or SAA meetings 2. Work the Twelve Steps, with a sponsor 3. Read literature (e.g., Diamond, 1988)
Mental illness	Evaluation by a mental health therapist who is also knowledgeable in Adult Child recovery
Physical illness	Evaluation by a physician knowledgeable in Adult Child recovery

While this chapter and this exercise
may look simple, actually doing it
and *working through it may not be easy*
and it *may take a lot of time.*

Whatever you have completed so far
in this chapter, if you have some time,
go to a quiet, comfortable and safe place
and begin to go inside, into your inner life,
where there are beliefs, thoughts, feelings,
somatic or physical sensations, possibilities,
creativities, intuitions, choices and experiences.

When you go into your own personal inner life,
what has come up for you while you've been
reading and working on this chapter?

The space below, if you choose,
is to write anything that might be coming up.

It may be helpful to take a break now.

15

A Full Recovery Program

Part 2

. . . Stage Two Recovery:
Using Group Therapy and Recovery Goals

After you have a stable or solid Stage One recovery
— regarding any Stage Zero conditions — you might want
to consider continuing to look around that toolbox.

Group Therapy

A **third tool** is **group therapy** that is specific for adult children
of troubled, unhealthy or dysfunctional families. Many
therapists and counselors who assist adult children in their
healing have found that for a number of reasons group therapy
is a helpful treatment aid and probably *the treatment of choice*
for adult children and for helping to heal our Child Within.

Some of these reasons are following and in the Appendix of *HCW.*

The Adult Child specific therapy group —

1. Is *safe.* While at times you may get some feedback that
   is uncomfortable, it is highly unlikely that you will be mistreated.
   The group generally follows principles of being safe.

2. Is *confidential.* Names and any identifying details of
   members and what goes on in the group stays in the group.

3. *Re-creates* many aspects of each member's *family of origin*
   and thus provides a vehicle to work through much
   unfinished business, such as painful emotional ties, conflicts
   and struggles (i.e., transference or projections) associated
   with their family of origin.

4. Provides each member with *several "therapists,"* instead
   of just one, as in individual therapy.

5. **Models recovery** in **various stages.** Especially motivating and healing is the ability to see people in beginning, middle and sometimes advanced stages of recovery. Many make definitive and at times dramatic positive changes in their lives and in healing their own Child Within.

6. With appropriately **trained** and **skilled group leaders,** the group is able to work on specific life issues that span the range of physical, mental, emotional, and spiritual recovery. I recommend *two* co-leaders who are not only trained and skilled in group, but who are well into healing their own Child Within.

7. Provides **supervision** and **guidance** in overall adult child recovery and healing.

8. Provides a **safe place to use** many of the **experiential techniques,** as described in Chapters 17 and 18.

9. Provides the well-known **advantages of group therapy in general,** such as the ability to obtain **identification, validation, feedback,** * **appropriate healing confrontation, support** and the many other useful factors and dynamics in group therapy.

The ideal therapy group size for such a group
is about eight or nine. The weekly fees
range across a spectrum of a sliding scale,
based on the person's income or ability to pay
(found usually only in a few funded agencies),
to fees that are in keeping with community standards (most groups).

---

*The most helpful, constructive and healing **feedback** in group may include any of the following . . .

- What I **see**
- What I **hear**

- How I can **identify** with you and
- What came up for me in **my inner life** when I heard your story.

Advice and suggestions are usually not as helpful, and defensiveness, judgment or attacks are often destructive.

Just like each individual group member,
each therapy group has its own personality.
I personally have led four of these groups
for over five years now, and I supervise an additional eight groups.

I have not seen any group with the same personality.*

Developing enough skills and momentum of self-healing to overcome and replace the negative conditioning, victim stance and repetition compulsion and to discover and heal our Child Within usually takes from *three to five years* of working such a *full recovery program*.

Recovery is not an intellectual or rational process. Nor is it easy.
It is an experiential process, consisting of excitement, discouragement, pain and joy, and with an overall pattern of personal growth. Recovery takes great courage.
Even though it cannot be explained adequately
with words alone, I have begun to describe this process of healing the Child Within in this book and in *HCW.*

Developing Recovery Goals

A **fourth tool** in recovery is **making** and **using** specific **goals** and objectives.

My co-leaders and I encourage, but do not force,
each group member to establish recovery goals,
updated every few months, that are specific
for their own needs and recovery.

To make these specific goals, I have developed a list
of general, generic or overall goals and guidelines for
Adult Children and co-dependent people.
(Co-dependence usually comes from growing up
in an unhealthy family and
all unrecovered Adult Children are co-dependent.
So these names are practically interchangeable.)

When you have some time, consider taking a look
at these. They are on the next page.

As you look at them, consider —
Are any of these goals interesting or desirable to me now?

What was it like for you to read these generic goals?
What came up for you in your inner life when you read them,
and what is coming up for you right now?
Write your responses on a separate page or in your diary or journal.

---

*I am not able to make referrals for people to therapy groups or to individual thera-pists in a specific geographic location.** I can outline an approach to seeking these out. (1) Ask around among your trusted friends and fellow recovering people. A good place to do that is at self-help meetings, especially Adult Children or Co-dependents Anonymous. (2) Call your local National Council on Alcoholism Office. (3) Look in the yellow pages under alcoholism, family or psychology. (4) Ask your individual therapist. See pages 115 and 129 in this book for more information. Also Bruckner-Gordon reference for more information on *individual* therapy.

Long-Term Recovery Goals
For Co-dependents And Adult Children

Self-Awareness

1. Discover, develop and accept my personal and individual identity as separate from spouse or partner, parental or other authority figure, children and institutions.)

2. Identify my ongoing needs (physical, mental, emotional and spiritual).

Self-Acceptance

3. Practice getting these needs met on my own and with safe people in healthy relationships.

4. Identify, trust and process my internal cues (feelings, sensations and experience from my inner life). If not comfortable, check my responses with someone I trust.

5. Assess my feelings, upsets, conflicts and similar situations and handle them in a healthy way (alone, with safe others and, if I choose, with my Higher Power).

6. Learn to accept myself as an individual and unique child of God, with strengths and weaknesses.

7. Learn to like myself and eventually to love myself, as my Higher Power loves me.

Self-Responsibility

8. Identify, re-experience and grieve the pain of ungrieved losses, hurts or mistreatment alone and with safe others.

9. Identify and work through my major core recovery issues.

10. Grieve the loss of my childhood while in group (for Adult Children).

11. Develop and use an ongoing support system (at least three supports).

Self-Reflection

12. There is no hurry for me to accomplish these goals right away. I can take my time.

13. I don't have to reach every goal perfectly.

14. I do not have to work on these goals in exactly this order.

15. From these above goals I will — in my own time — make more specific and more personal goals for myself during my recovery.

16. I can accomplish these goals through techniques such as risking and telling my story to safe people, through prayer and meditation, keeping a journal and other experiential techniques.

17. Using the above, I am caring for and healing my true self.

As I assist an Adult Child in recovery in healing their Child Within, I encourage, but do not force them to begin thinking about specific problems or conditions in their life that they would like to improve or change.

From listing these problems or conditions, they then create specific goals or what they want to happen.

And from these specific goals, they create a specific plan or method of just how they will reach these goals.

I show some examples below.

Table 15.1. Sample Treatment or Recovery Plan

My Problems	What I Want to Happen (Goals)	How I Plan to Reach these Goals
Chronic unhappiness	Experience some happiness and serenity	1. Begin to heal my Child Within 2. Make a commitment to an Adult Child specific therapy group long term
Low self-esteem	Raise my self-esteem	3. Attend that group weekly and work on a personal problem or issue at least monthly 4. Whenever it comes up, share about my low self-esteem and shame
Difficulty with intimate relationships	Improve my participation in my intimate relationships Have one successful intimate relationship	1. Practice 1 to 4 above 2. Work on my relationship problems in group therapy 3. Keep a diary or journal about my experiences in relationships 4. Seek individual therapy with a therapist knowledgeable in Adult Child recovery.

On the next page is space to write your own personal
recovery plan to assist in healing your Child Within.

Take as much time as you need to think about,
consider and write whatever comes up for you.

If you are in counseling, therapy or a therapy group now,
it would be helpful in your healing process
to **share these goals** with your therapist or group
and ask them to support you as you work through them.
You could also **ask for feedback and suggestions.**

Keep a copy of your recovery plan handy
and read it carefully every week or two.
Each time ask yourself, "What can I do to facilitate my
achieving these healing methods and goals?"

Every three or four months it is useful to review your plan
and add to, subtract from or change it in any way that you choose.
Then review it with your group or therapist.

Healing by Working through Conflict (see also pages 142-148)

At times in long-term group or individual therapy a conflict
may develop in the group wherein you may feel uncomfortable.

It is useful for you to know that in all likelihood,
going into and working through this conflict will be
a healing and growing experience for you.

During this time, and at other times,
as you get progressively more into being aware of
your feelings, you **may hurt** so much,
through such feelings as fear, sadness, shame,
anger and/or confusion, that you may want to
terminate being in the group or in individual therapy.

It is at this time when you have an opportunity to learn to

- **tolerate emotional pain more clearly,** and

- **work through conflict.**

Chart 15.1. My Recovery Goals and Methods

My Problems	What I Want to Happen (Goals)	How I Plan to Reach these Goals

It is especially healing to tell your group
and/or your individual therapist, if you choose,
about *everything* that comes up for you around all of this.

When a person is in group or individual therapy,
they always have possibilities and choices
related to their Adult Child recovery and to
healing their Child Within.

There may come a time when the person
gets so discouraged, frustrated or impatient
that in an all-or-none fashion they leave the group or therapist
without discussing with them how they are feeling.

When this happens, not only is it somewhat disruptive
to the group and to the healing process, but the person's
Inner Child usually goes even deeper into hiding.

To help prevent this, it is usually healing to discuss it in
group or individual over a period of several weeks or longer.

Some possible actions in such a situation might include

- Terminate therapy

- Stay and work through the pain and conflict

- Work through it, then "take a breather"
  by not actively working on any personal
  issues for a time, while still attending group regularly.

- Some other possibility _____

_____

(fill in the blank)

It is precisely at these times of frustration
that we can heal our Child Within
even more than had we left group or individual therapy
without working through our pain and conflict.
So, in a sense, these could actually be exciting
times of opportunity, healing and growth.

In the past some of us may have run away from pain
and conflict and/or "beat ourself up" over it, stuffing our pain.

*It is in the safety and support of
group and/or individual therapy that we
can learn to tolerate emotional pain more clearly,
work through conflict
and grow from it.*

As you read and reflect on the above material
what in your inner life is coming up for you?

Terminating from Group Therapy

Somewhere in the course of the three to five years or more
in group therapy you may wonder about or even sense
that you may be ready to terminate group therapy.

A constructive and healing way to proceed
would include the following:

- Reviewing the generic, long-term recovery goals (page 118),
  estimate about how far you had reached each goal, on a scale
  from 0 to 10, just *before you started group therapy,* and write
  that number in the space to the left of the goal. Then estimate
  about where you sense that you are *right now* in reaching that
  goal, and write it in the space just to the right of the goal. Show
  that to your group members and leaders, and ask for feedback
  on where each of them senses that you are *right now.*

- Do the same with your specific personal recovery goals (page 121).

- Review the overall criteria for healing the Child Within on page 246, and do the same with these. These are a bit more stringent than these above goals, and may be more than you can do right now.

- Ask your group and leaders for feedback about your recovery in general and whether they sense it would be an appropriate time for you to leave group therapy now.

Take at least four to six weeks for this entire process. There is no need to rush through any of this.

If you have reached in the neighborhood of 90% of the way, or 9 out of a scale of 10 in your goals in experiencing the healing you wanted, and if the group and leaders' sense is that termination for you is appropriate right now, then you may consider terminating from group.

When you do so, it is useful to have at least three *strong support systems* that are ongoing in your life. Tell the group about these and how you plan to use them.

It is also entirely appropriate and healthy to return for brief individual counseling or therapy whenever you sense the need. You may also return to group therapy later if you feel the need for more healing work in a group. As you reflect upon any of the above, feel free to write about what may be coming up for you on some extra paper.

Other Group Experiences

A **fifth tool** is **educational group** experience. These may consist of several sessions where didactic material on the Adult Child syndrome or co-dependence is presented by a therapist, counselor or teacher. They may also include some experiential exercises and some brief group interactions.

While these are not meant to be formal group therapy, they can be helpful in cognitive learning and in beginning to learn to heal with others, which can be of some assistance in helping us to heal our Child Within.

If you are considering participating in one of these, or if you have already started or completed one, you can use some extra paper for writing anything that may come up for you around this.

16

A Full Recovery Program

Part 3
Stage Two Recovery Continued:
. . . Self-Help Groups, Individual Therapy
and Other Recovery Tools

A **sixth tool** is a **self-help group** —

Those oriented to helping heal the adult child condition
and co-dependence include the fellowships of:

- Al-Anon (or Nar-Anon)

- Adult Children Anonymous (or . . . of Alcoholics
  or . . . of Dysfunctional Families) and

- Co-dependents Anonymous (CoDA)

Each of these uses the universal Twelve Steps
and Twelve Traditions, borrowed from AA,
as the basis of their recovery "program."
Meetings are free of charge, last about one hour
and the size consists of from two people (rarely) to 50 or more.

A secretary usually reads a preamble
and introduction, then there is sharing
of personal stories, experience, strength and hope.

People usually do not use their last names
and in this way the meetings are anonymous.

"Cross-talk" or direct feedback during the meeting
is generally and wisely discouraged;
this differs from group therapy,
where the healing aid of feedback is facilitated
by the two group leaders and by observations and
the recovery experience of the other group members.

These Twelve-Step programs have many uses,
including sharing, identifying, fellowship and
program structure, guidance and work.

Getting a Sponsor

It is useful to get a sponsor (same gender)
who has more recovery than you
and with whom you feel comfortable,
and use them to assist you in working the Twelve Steps.
As is true with all human beings,
the healing and humility of sponsors vary,
so if you sense that you are not growing
or are being misdirected or even mistreated (this is uncommon),
you may wish to terminate with that sponsor
and find another. However, what sometimes
feels like mistreatment *now* may actually be
more *useful in our healing* as a *reminder to* us
of a past mistreatment,
the conflict and grief of which we might not
have yet worked through.
It is here that the experience, expertise and wisdom
of a therapy group and/or a therapist
can be helpful in helping us sort these things out.

As we attend these self-help meetings and
as we work the Twelve Steps with our sponsor,
it can then be useful to **integrate**
our knowledge and wisdom from these experiences
with our knowledge and wisdom from the other methods
of healing described in this book and elsewhere,
and especially the recovery aid of group therapy.

The general focus in **Al-Anon** (or **Nar-Anon**)
is getting free of the unnecessary pain and suffering
from living with or being close in a relationship
with an alcoholic (or other drug-dependent person).

The general focus in **Adult Children Anonymous,**
or the like, is on recognizing and sharing
experiences around family of origin issues and
getting free of unnecessary pain and suffering around these.

The general focus in **Co-dependents Anonymous**
is on getting free of unnecessary pain and suffering*
in relationships, whether they be past or current.

On the next page is a table that
at first glance looks complicated.
In this table I describe and compare
some of the various characteristics of all three
self-help programs, as well as group therapy,
individual therapy, short-term intensive experiences,
and workshops, conferences and educational groups.
Listing 16 different characteristics vertically along the side,
I compare these on a scale of from zero (none)
to 1 (minimal or some) to 4 (maximal or most).
I also add comments about each, where appropriate.

Take as much time as you need with the table
to look over the characteristics of
each of these recovery methods.

Know that these numbers and comments are
only approximate and are only the opinions
of myself and some colleagues whom I respect.
But they might assist you in getting started
if you want to know a little more comparatively
about these various recovery aids.

---

*I discuss unnecessary pain and suffering in general and how to get free of it in specific
workshops on core issues and in more detail in my book in process, *Wisdom to Know the
Difference.*

Table 16.1. Characteristics of Recovery Methods for Adult Children of Dysfunctional Families and for Co-dependents

	Methods							
	Al-Anon	ACA Self-help	Co-dependents Anonymous	Group Therapy (Inter-actional)	Individual Psycho-therapy	Short Term Intensive Treatment	Workshops Conferences & Educa-tional Groups	No Recovery Program
Potential For Personal Growth	1-2	2	2-3	1-4	1-3	2-3	1	0-1
Meeting Size	2-100+	2-100+	2-100+	7-10	2	10-30	Small to Large	0
Length of Meeting	1 hour	1 hour	1 hour	1¼-2 hours	30-50 minutes	Multiple & Vary	Varies	0
Consistency of Attendance by Others	1-3	1-2	1-3	3-4	4	4 (Short Term Only)	Varies	0
Frequency of Meeting	Daily Possible	Weekly to Daily Possible	Weekly or More	Weekly	As Scheduled	Daily Short Term	Short Term	0
Professional Therapists	0	0	0	Yes	Yes	Yes	Varies	0
Supervision in Overall Recovery	1-2	1-2	1-2	3-4	1-3	2-3	0-1	0
Fee	0	0	0	Yes	Yes	Yes	Yes	0
Depth of Shared Feelings	1-2	2-3	2-3	2-4	1-4	2-4	0-2	0-1

Level of Intimacy	1-2	1-3	1-3	2-4	1-3	2-4	1-2	0-1
Confidentiality	1-3	1-3	1-3	3-4	4	3-4	0-1	0-4
Healthy Family Modeled	1-2	1-3	1-3	3-4	1-2	3	1-2	0+
Feedback	0-1	0-1	0-1	2-4	1-4	2-4	1-2	0
Suggested Duration of Attendance	Long Term	Long Term	Long Term	3-5 years	As Needed	Short/Long Term Program Needed	Short Term	0
Commitment to Attend	0	0	0	Long Term	Varies	Yes	Varies	0
Availability of Long Term Support	As Available	As Available	As Available	Yes	As Scheduled	0	0	0
COMMENTS	Focus: Relationships with alcoholics. Teaches detachment and self-awareness.	Focus: Family of origin work. Awareness and expression of feelings.	Focus: Relationships past and current and awareness of self.	Co-leaders' specific experience and personal recovery of therapist is important.	Specific experience and personal recovery of the therapist is crucial. Ask around and test your intuition and personal growth in the therapy.	Varies from residential 5-30 days to weekends to "reconstruction." Long-term recovery program is up to the individual and may be weak. Can be dangerous if used alone.	Useful for awakening and general information. Supplements other recovery methods. Frustrating if used alone long term.	Depends on individual. Full recovery rare, if ever. Can enter any recovery method at any time.

COMMENTS (left panel):

For guidelines on recovery, see Gravitz & Bowden 1985, Whitfield 1987, 88, Subby 1987. Most experts agree that group therapy is the treatment of choice for adult children and for co-dependent people, supplemented by other methods shown here.

Useful for sharing, identifying, program structure and fellowship. Advice from others varies from excellent to poor. Work the program. Get a sponsor. Integrate these self-help group experiences with other methods as described here and elsewhere (see panel to left), especially group therapy.

Key: 0 = none   1 = minimal or some   4 = maximal or most

After this introduction to these self-help groups and other recovery aids, is anything coming up for you around any of this? If so, and if you wish, here is a space to write about that.

Feel like taking a break now?

Individual Counseling or Therapy

A **seventh tool** is
individual counseling or therapy which can be helpful in healing our Child Within.
Some indications for individual counseling include

- I would like to work more on my recovery than the time available for me in my therapy group.

- I have issues to work on that I do not yet feel comfortable talking about in my therapy group. For example, sexual issues, incest, extremely embarrassing issues, and the like.

- I feel somehow blocked in my work in group therapy and want to explore that outside as well as inside group.

- I just *want* to work on my recovery in individual therapy.

Individual therapy or counseling may last for as short as one session through a range of a few sessions to as long as many sessions. How long depends on a number of things — including what you want to work on and what you'd like to happen.

While you don't need to have your
problems and **goals** clarified to begin, it can be helpful
and save you money and time
for you to *know something* about these *before* you begin.

It is most important to determine if your
therapist is qualified to assist
you in **what you want to accomplish.**

One way to begin that process is to find
a therapist who
- Knows the principles of adult child recovery,
  co-dependence and addiction recovery,
  as well as psychotherapy in general.
- Knows how to assist people in healing
  their Child Within, and
- Is well advanced into their own adult child recovery
  and healing their own Child Within.

Ask someone you trust to give you some names of therapists
and then if you have enough time and money,
interview two or three people and see
who you sense might fit best.
You need *not* be intimidated by pressure
or promises, or impressed by degrees or certification
(though the latter two may help in your decision).

As you search, you may consider writing the names of therapists
you interview and any comments about your reaction and your
sense of their expertise, ability and compassion in assisting you as
you work on your issue or issues.

Chart 16.1. Checklist for Therapist Interviews

Name	Comments after Interview

If you cannot afford a regular fee,* you may want to explore seeing a skilled therapist who works at a community mental health center in your area. Ask around or look in the telephone book to locate them.

If someone comes highly recommended, and after your interview with them you sense they can help you, you may not need to interview any more people. You could always interview others if you sense that they don't end up being of help.

When you work to heal yourself with a therapist or counselor, you can avoid several traps that can block your ability to heal your Child Within. Here are six "Don'ts" — things to avoid — so that your recovery may go better. Regarding your therapist, counselor, or group leader —

Try not to
- expect they can "fix" you with their "magical powers."
- be their friend, and don't expect them to be yours.
- tell them what you think they want to hear.
- tell them part truths or part secrets about yourself.
- try to seduce them in any way,
  including giving them gifts or the like.
- rehearse the exact words that you'll say
  (it is useful, however, to *plan what
  you want to work on).*

The solution to using your therapist or group for your best healing is to **be real** with them. Tell them exactly what is in your **inner life as it comes up** for you.

Many of the principles for working in *group* therapy apply to working in individual therapy, as I have indicated on pages 115 through 124.

It is common and appropriate to have feelings such as fear, embarrassment or shame, guilt, confusion and the like around beginning any kind of recovery aid, especially including individual or group therapy. If you have any similar feelings or if you have beliefs that you may have learned from parents, peers or anywhere that going to counseling means you are weak, bad, or crazy, it may be helpful to write about that and talk about it with someone safe.

---

*You will be expected to pay their fee for the initial or evaluation interview.

Intensive Residential Or Weekend Experiences

An **eighth tool** is **intensive** weekend or longer residential **experiences**. These can be helpful in healing our Child Within in several circumstances, including:

- A marked dysfunction or crisis that cannot be managed by adult child specific outpatient treatment.*
- Difficulty working and growing in adult child specific outpatient treatment, which ideally includes group therapy.
- Continued difficulty identifying and expressing feelings in an adult child specific recovery program.
- Worked well and grew initially, and now in a prolonged lull.
- Persistent minimizing or denying of family of origin issues.
- Needs some more time to work than is available in group, and/or
- Wants to have an intensive residential experience.

Ask your peers, group members and therapists
to tell you any of *their* experiences at any of these.
The focus of these experiences should be
adult child or co-dependence recovery or healing the Child Within.**

Although health insurance usually does not pay for these experiences, unfortunately, I have heard many people say they were one of the best experiences of their life. If anything in your inner life is coming up around any of the above, write about it on a separate sheet or in your journal.

---

*Some people who are especially dysfunctional may benefit for up to 30 days or longer in a hospital or residential facility that uses an adult child, co-dependence, or healing the Child Within focus. Some health insurance plans may pay for part or most of this treatment.

A Caution: While these are generally healing experiences, they can be disruptive to your life functioning in general if you do not have the concomitant and ongoing support of a therapy group or individual therapy. I do *not* recommend that these experiences be used alone, without ongoing group or individual therapy for at least several months after the experience. This is to help facilitate a healthy integration of these often powerful experiences into your healing and into your life. If you attend such an experience, there is also a danger of "comparing out" a less intense and slower paced outpatient recovery program because in the intensive experience the "hit" of emotional experience and freedom can be so intense, almost like that of a drug. Such "comparing out" can end up blocking your long-term healing. (This can be an especially dangerous trap for people with a strong history of addictions.) If any of this happens for you, discuss it with your therapy group and/or therapist.

Time Alone

A final equally *important* and *powerful* **tool** for healing
is constructive **time alone** or solitude.

While a major issue for us adult children
is difficulty with intimate relationships
until we know and are comfortable with our True Self,
our Child Within, any satisfying intimate relationship
with another will likely be difficult for us.

My experience of the way we heal our Child Within
is that it is in **three relationships: with ourself,**
safe others and, if we choose, **our Higher Power.**
These relationships are the basis for my and
others' beginning definition of what spirituality is about.

There may be only two relationships
that we can never escape for very long —
that with ourself and with our Higher Power.

Every relationship that we experience
involves our awareness of our True Self.
If we do not know experientially what is going on
within it in our inner life, we will likely not be able
to relate fully to others, the world and to our Higher Power.

So it is useful in recovery to spend time alone,
just getting to know our True Self better.

But sometimes the pain of being alone
can feel almost unbearable and we may
compulsively rush out to be with other people.
Or we may self-medicate with other things, such as work,
sex, eating, alcohol, other drugs, spending money, gambling
and the like — anything that may lessen our pain.

As you are reading this, if you have time now, go inside for a minute
or two. What is coming up for you right now?

In his book *Solitude: A Return to the Self,*
Anthony Storr writes,

> The burden of value with which we are at present loading interpersonal relationships is too heavy for those fragile craft to carry. Our expectation that satisfying intimate relationships should, ideally, provide happiness and that if they do not, there must be something wrong with those relationships, seems to be exaggerated.

> Love and friendship are, of course, an important part of what makes life worthwhile. But they are not the only source of happiness. Moreover, human beings change and develop as life goes on . . .

> Many ordinary interests and the majority of creative pursuits involving real origina ity continue without involving relationships. It seems to me that what goes on in the human being when he is by himself is as important as what happens in his interactions with other people . . .

> The creative person is constantly seeking to discover himself, to remodel his own identity and to find meaning in the universe by means of what he creates. He finds this to be a valuable integrating process which, like meditation or prayer, has little to do with other people but which has its own separate validity. His most significant moments are those in which he attains some new insight, or makes some new discovery; and these moments are chiefly, if not invariably, those in which he is alone.

I've seen many people who I've assisted
in their healing and recovery who use people, places and things
to self-medicate their pain of being alone.
At times I've suggested or "prescribed" that
they start by spending just 30 minutes each day alone
with no distractions. They can meditate, write in
their journal, or in other ways be with themselves,
but otherwise, no distractions.
Many have much difficulty doing that
and that difficulty, that pain, is then useful
grist for the mill of their work in therapy and recovery.

If being alone in that way seems painful
for you, it might be something to try.
Alone, with no distractions, the Child Within
sometimes feels safe enough to come out.
If you have any doubts or concerns
about trying this experience of being alone,
talk it over with your therapy group,
therapist or another safe person.

Should you decide to try it, you might
do so once and see how that feels.
Then try it at least once a day for a few days
and experience how that feels.

Feel free to write in the space below
anything that may come up for you during
any of these times.

Would you like to take a break now?

We Do the Work

In using each of these recovery aids to help us heal our Child Within, we, the individual, do the work of recovery.

Others are there to assist us and to support us.

We do not have to recover alone,
and the only way we can recover
is by our own internal resources.
Those internal resources are the sensitive, vulnerable
and powerful dimensions of
the inner life of the Child Within itself.

In their own imperfections, the other people involved in
these recovery aids may frustrate us to go within,
gently unearth and begin to nurture that little Child.

Is there anything that is coming up for you now that you would like to write about or to talk about? If there is, here is some space.

Would you like to take a break now?

Notes

17

Experiencing

...Introduction and Working Through
Conflict and Transference

My best guess is that about 90%
of healing our Child Within, of Adult Child recovery,
is **experiential** — in the realm of our personal experience.
And about 10% of our healing and recovery
is cognitive, in the realm of our intellect and mental understanding.
That is one reason why I created this book.

Originally I wrote my first book *Healing the Child Within*
to help organize and explain what I was seeing
in people's personal healing and recovery. I wanted to
pass that information on to anyone who might be interested.

Over the first two years of its publication
people gave me a lot of positive feedback on *HCW*
about their healing experiences while reading it
and using its ideas in their own personal recoveries.

During that time I also continued to personally observe
the recoveries of over 100 people in the adult child specific
therapy groups that I co-led, and those of a smaller number
of people who I saw in individual counseling.
I also supervised the group leaders of several
additional AC therapy groups.

While I knew and still believe that it works most effectively
for each of us to initiate, work through
and create **our own** healing and recovery,
I sensed that there was more that I could add that would
help explain the healing power of **experiencing** our recovery.
Assisting and seeing my people work through their healing
in an experiential and cognitive way,
I wanted to put together in a readable,
understandable and **experience-able** way
what it can be like to heal our Child Within.
That is this book, *A Gift To Myself*.

Like recovery and like life,
a person can *experience* this book
on one or more of several **levels.**

- The first is **reading** some, most or even all of this book,
  but having little or no experiential response.
  The reader might feel some numbness,
  and although some degree of pain, joy or excitement
  might try to arise, they may hold it back.
  Or they might let in some pain, but no joy or excitement.

- Another level is while reading it, to **feel** some pain, fear,
  joy, excitement or other feelings,
  but choosing not to do any of the experiential exercises,
  and perhaps not to write anything down.

- A third level is to begin **writing** some personal reactions,
  and perhaps even to do one or more of the exercises.

- A fourth level is to **do** most or even all
  of the exercises, but not otherwise participate
  in a recovery program.

- A fifth level is to do the **exercises** *and* to participate
  in a partial or even a **full recovery program**
  for healing our Child Within.

The powerful thing about all of these
levels or possibilities is that we can *choose* to do
or not do any one of these now
and at any moment in our lives.

When we were very young and little,
we may not have known about these possibilities
and these choices.

Now we do.

We are learning that we have options
and progressively more possibilities and choices,
as we get to know and be our True Self.

Experiencing

When we experience, we are in
that powerful part of us that we call
our inner life.
Our inner life includes our beliefs, thoughts, memories,
feelings, body sensations, intuitions, possibilities, choices
and decisions, all in the precise moment of now.
So if you are experiencing any of these aspects
of your inner life right now
and are focused, with no distractions,
you are *experiencing*.

A goal in healing our Child Within
is to continue experiencing that inner life,
which is a major part of the Child,
as much as we possibly can. Eventually we can learn that
when our false or adapted or co-dependent self
comes in and takes over, we just notice that,
and then decide whether we need
that false self right now or not.

The false self was the way we learned to survive the pain.
When we were growing up,
we didn't always have much of a choice.
No one taught us the difference.
And so now, sometimes we might still
have a hard time knowing the difference.

Experiential Techniques

A way we can begin to experience
our powerful inner life more and more
is to choose one or more experiential techniques
that may help facilitate our experiencing.

If you have had any kind of reaction
other than no reaction at all or numbness
just from reading and/or working in this book,
you are already using an experiential technique.

Experiential healing techniques tend to have
some of the following characteristics in common:

- **Being Real** — we tend to be our Real
  or True Self when we are using them,
  although in the beginning we feel uncomfortable.
- **Focused** — we are focused on an aspect of
  our inner life.
- **Structured** — there is a structure or form
  to the technique itself, and
- **Safe** — to be most healing, it is generally
  done in a safe and supportive environment.

As feelings come up, we can share them with
one or more appropriate, safe people, and then
work through them toward a healthy resolution.

On the next page I list 21 varieties
of experiential techniques that can be useful
in healing our Child Within.

Although I will briefly describe some of these techniques,
if you have any questions about any of them,
it would be most helpful to ask a safe person,
such as a therapist who has training and experience in
adult child recovery and healing the Child Within.

If you are in an adult child specific therapy group,
it would also be constructive to ask your
group members and group leaders for further information.

Also group therapy is an ideal and safe place
to *practice* many of these experiential techniques.

Some Experiential Techniques For
Healing Our Child Within

1. *Risking* and *sharing*, especially feelings,
   with safe and supportive people.
2. *Storytelling (telling our own story,*
   including risking and sharing).
3. *Working through transference* (what we project or
   "transfer" onto others, and vice versa for them).
4. *Psychodrama* and its variations: Reconstruction,
   Gestalt Therapy and Family Sculpture.
5. *Hypnosis* and related techniques.
6. Attending *Self-Help Meetings*.
7. *Working the Twelve Steps* (of ACA, Al-Anon, CoDA,
   AA, NA, OA, etc.).
8. *Group Therapy* (usually a safe and supportive place to
   practice many of these experiential techniques).
9. *Couples Therapy* or *Family Therapy*
10. *Guided Imagery*
11. *Breathwork*
12. *Affirmations*
13. *Dream Analysis*
14. *Art, Movement* and *Play Therapy*
15. *Active Imagination, Using Intuition,* and *Voice Dialogue*
16. *Meditation* and *Prayer*
17. *Therapeutic Bodywork*
18. *Keeping a journal* or a *diary*
19. *Writing an unmailed letter*
20. Using a *workbook like this*
21. *Creating our own* experiential techniques or healing.

These experiential techniques ideally should be used
in the context of a full recovery program,
as described throughout this book,
and especially in Chapters 14, 15 and 16.

A therapist with training and experience in assisting people with
one or more of these techniques can be helpful.
Most therapists and counselors do not have training and expertise
in working with all of these methods. If you have any doubt, ask
your therapist outright.

I will now briefly describe and make some comments on each of
these.

Experiential Techniques — Some Comments

1. **Risking and sharing,** especially feelings,
   with safe and supportive people, can facilitate
   our contacting our Child Within.
   This can be done with anyone who is safe and supportive.

2. **Telling our own story,** which includes the risking and sharing
   mentioned above, can likewise help us contact and
   be our True Self. I discuss these first two experiences
   further in Chapter 21, page 187.

3. **Working through transference.** Transference is unconscious
   material that we conjure up about or sense is in others
   that is actually a feeling or an issue that is incomplete in ourself.

This feeling or issue is usually one that reminds us
of an old hurt or conflict that we never resolved
or healed and is thus "unfinished business."
And so we project or "transfer" aspects of our unhealed hurts,
wishes or conflicts onto the other person. That is in large part why
family members and other *close people,* who are
themselves unhealed, transfer so much onto us,
and why we may transfer so much onto them
and onto other people who are close to us.

Therapy and counseling offer the advantage
of being a safe place to transfer and to work on
and heal our unhealed hurt, traumas and conflicts.
In individual counseling or therapy we have **one** person
with whom we can do this healing work.
When our therapist, being human also, has similar
issues come up, it is called *countertransference.*

The therapist may work a bit on his or her own transference issues,
or countertransference, in the therapy session with you,
but will likely work most on them with a supervising
therapist used specifically for this purpose. This is because
for your best healing the focus should be kept on you.
For co-leaders in a therapy group, they may
use one another in this supervising capacity.

In *group therapy* we have an additional healing advantage.
We have as many people as are in the group
with whom we can work on and heal our unfinished business.
And this number includes the group leaders.

For example, when they are "treating us" the way we want
them to — and the way we wanted our parents to treat us
— the group leaders may represent a "good parent" to us.
When a group leader makes a mistake or
somehow doesn't give us what we want,
they may represent a "bad parent" to us.
That is, we transfer feelings and conflicts
that are unhealed for us onto them.
Or an older man group member may likewise feel to us
like a bad father or an older woman seem
like a bad mother to us.
Or another man may feel like our brother who
mistreated us, or another woman member of the group
may feel to us like our sister who mistreated us.
And so, likewise, we may transfer
our unresolved feelings and conflicts onto any of them.
We may also transfer "positive" feelings and issues onto others.

One common result from "negative" transference is

CONFLICT

And conflict nearly always **hurts.**
And a part of us wants to stop it from happening.
At this point we are right in the *experience*
of the experiential method that *we have created*
with the assistance of the group and its leaders
(or the therapist, if we are in individual therapy).

If you have time now, take a few minutes,
and imagine yourself in such a conflict.
What might you be **feeling**? And what **possibilities** and
choices might you have to handle this conflict?

Before you read the next page, if you choose, write in
your journal or elsewhere any of your responses.

Transference offers us the opportunity to examine our *unconscious* beliefs, thoughts, feelings, and decisions in a
safe, therapeutic setting.

We might be tempted to blame the person
or persons with whom we are in conflict
and to flee the group or individual therapy.
As I mentioned on pages 120 and 122 of Chapter 15, however,
we may have far more healing possibilities and choices
than leaving therapy in an all-or-none fashion,
which would likely only send our Child Within
deeper into hiding and strengthen our false self.

As I describe in *Wisdom to Know the Difference,*
at this point it can be useful to examine
at least **three levels** on which we can work
when we are **in any conflict.**

1. The first is the most obvious — the conflict we have
   with the person or people *in our life right here and now.*
   Depending on several factors,
   the meaning of our differences with the other or others may vary
   from minor to major in the actual dynamics of
   the particular conflict. But no matter what these are,
   we will likely have to work through this level
   to arrive at a resolution. If the issue exists only at this level,
   it should be relatively easy to resolve.

2. The second level takes us deeper into our True Self,
   perhaps even into its **unconscious,**
   that part of us about which we are unaware right now.
   At this level our conflict may not be so much
   with the person(s) at level one, but with a person
   or **people from our past** and with whom we have not
   been able to work through a conflict that is similar to
   the conflict in level one. At this level
   our feelings are intense and often overwhelming.
   Common sense resolution escapes us.

   To help us become more aware of this kind
   of unfinished business, we might ask ourself
   the following question —

   > **Of whom or what from my past does
   > or might this conflict** (from level one) **remind me?**

   We might then tell someone safe or write
   our answers to this healing question.

If we are reminded of anyone or of any specific experience,
we can then begin to work on answering some of the following:

- **With whom was the conflict?**

- **When was it?**

- **How old was I?**

- **What happened?**

- **And what happened next?**

- **And what happened after that?**

- **Did I ever try to resolve it? How?**

- **And is there any way for me to get free
  of this unfinished conflict?**

On the next two pages I have made an outline of these
levels and questions for you to use in helping
to resolve these kinds of conflicts.
Depending on the conflict, its duration and the others involved,
it may take us days to weeks to months
or even longer to work through an unfinished conflict.
It is helpful to take as much time as we need.
While there is often pain associated with it,
there is usually no rush to resolve this conflict.
Use your therapy group, therapist and/or journal to assist
in your work around any such conflict.

3. The final level may be still deeper.
   This includes *painful material* or *patterns* that we may have
   stuffed or repressed into our unconscious mind
   that we may still *believe* about ourself (i.e., **old tapes**).
   These are usually related in some important way
   to the conflict in the first two levels and thus
   may also be important in resolving the conflict.

   To help us become more aware of this level
   of unfinished business, we might ask ourself
   the following questions —

Chart 17.1. Checklist to Aid in Resolving a Conflict

Level of Conflict	What is the conflict about?	What are my feelings and other Inner Life around the conflict?
1 With Person or People or Situation Here and Now		
2 With Past Unhealed or Unfinished Conflict		
3 Painful or Negative Messages, Material or Patterns Resulting from Past Conflict		

This is a lot of material to consider. Give yourself plenty of time to work through any of it. Anytime you wish, including when you have completed it, use extra paper to write about what this work may be bringing up for you. Take regular breaks from it, especially if you feel overwhelmed. Make extra blank copies of this chart for future use.

Some Clarifying Questions	Some possible Answers, Meanings and Solutions to the Conflict
Importance of conflict to me? Minor? Moderate? Major? What would it mean and/or result in if I were to resolve this conflict? What do I want to happen? What would I have to give up to get what I want to happen?	
Of whom or what does this conflict in level 1 *remind* me? Who was it with? When was it? How old was I? What happened? What happened next? After that? Did I ever try to resolve it? How? Any way to get free of this unfinished conflict now? How have I worked on this conflict in my therapy group, individual session or journal now?	
What rigid rules or negative messages did I hear or learn around this past conflict? What beliefs, belief systems or negative attitudes did I form around this past conflict? What aspects or part of the person(s) in the past conflict might I have incorporated or taken in? How have I worked on this conflict in my therapy group, individual session or journal now?	

- **What rigid rules or negative messages
  did I hear or learn around this past conflict?**

- **What beliefs, belief systems or attitudes
  did I form around this past conflict?**

- **What aspect or part of the person(s) in this past conflict
  might I have incorporated or taken in
  as though it were now part of myself?**

- **What aspect or part of the person(s) in this past conflict
  might I have incorporated or taken in
  as though it were now part of myself?**

We might then tell a safe person and *write* our answers
to these healing questions.

And as with the previous levels, we can use
our group, therapist or journal to assist
in our work around this level of our conflict.

On the previous two pages is an outline that may be useful
in working through such a conflict.
For future use before writing on these, consider making some
extra copies of them for use in helping resolve future conflicts.

Remember that while a help, this two-page chart is not a final
solution to resolving conflicts and transference issues.

Depending on the *person* with whom I am in conflict,
how *safe* and *available* they are and how *committed*
I feel to the relationship, I *may* or may *not* be able
and/or want to work on this conflict *directly* with them.

No matter what, I can work on it in group therapy,
individual therapy, in my journal or in some other safe way.

If such transference issues come up, I can now possibly feel more
familiar and less uneasy with working through them.

It is our Child Within or True Self who does the work
in resolving conflicts and in working through transference.
It is generally our false self or negative ego
that contributes to the *formation* of the conflict.
However, that false self or ego may also be
a friend in disguise at times, as it might be trying
to tell us something important or to help us survive.

Infatuation with Your Therapist

There is another important kind of transference
that is fairly common, especially in
individual counseling or therapy, and that is
becoming infatuated with our therapist.

Rather than being "true love," this "positive" transference
nearly always means that we are projecting
onto the therapist or other helping professional
many of the healing qualities that we have
already inherent within ourself, but we do not know that we do.
We may also be projecting our wish for
unconditional love from our parents.

This kind of transference is potentially dangerous.
Not only can it *block our healing,*
but if the therapist breaks the ethical code
and gets into any kind of physical and/or emotional
"affair" with us, the wheels are now in motion
for us to be *further mistreated and wounded.*
Aside from being unethical practice by the therapist,
this may have the devastating effect of
discouraging us from all future attempts at healing,
and our Child Within may remain in hiding indefinitely.

Probably less than 5% of therapists are themselves
unhealed in this kind of situation.
Rather than facilitate your healing work
through the transference, they may —
coming from their own countertransference or from simple lust —
try to initiate a physical and/or emotional affair with you.
But there is *never* a justification for doing that.
It will inevitably damage your Child Within.

To help prevent these dangerous consequences
and to protect our Child Within,
we can risk *talking about it* with our therapist
when even the first hint of it comes up.

The therapist or counselor — or helping professional
of any kind — should be trained to recognize
and to deal with this positive transference
in a way that is most healing to you.
In this situation you are vulnerable.
Before any such "affair," or even a *hint* of one,
and before any of these other destructive consequences,
it is the responsibility of the therapist
to use this transference to assist you in working through any
associated conflicts and in discovering your own inner strengths.

You can trust nearly all therapists to be ethical,
responsible and to safely facilitate your work
through the real conflict underneath the transference.

Some people who may be especially vulnerable
to being mistreated or abused by their therapist
in this way are those who have been **physically**
or **sexually abused** as children, adolescents,
or even as adults, and others
who have **blurred** personal **boundaries.**

If you come close to having such an affair,
it is then healing to find a safe person
with whom to talk and process your experience.
While you may be reluctant to do so, at this point
it can be constructive to search out a new therapist
to continue the work of healing your Child Within.

Has anything even remotely like *any* of the above
ever happened to you?
What happened?
What came up in your inner life?
How did you handle it?
What has come up for you around this since then
and how did you handle that?
Would you be interested in writing whatever you wish
on some extra paper?

If a helping professional of any kind has been sexually
inappropriate with you, you may consider taking some
form of legal action and/or notifying his or her
professional association, society, or state licensing board.

Would you like to take a break now?

18

Continuing To Experience

In the previous chapter I began to discuss
the healing effect of *experiencing* as we recover.
I also reviewed the first three of 21 methods
that may facilitate our learning and re-learning
how to experience our True Self, our Child Within.
Because of their crucial importance in recovery,
I spent some time on the frequent experiences of transference
(or projection) and conflict in our recovery.

In this chapter I will continue reviewing some of
the remaining aids to our experiencing and healing.

4. **Psychodrama** and its variations: **Gestalt therapy,
   Family Sculpture** and **Family Reconstruction,**
   can facilitate our experiencing several aspects
   of our healing process, such as —
   - What happened
   - How we were misparented and mistreated
   - What came up for us in our inner life
   - *When* in time the above happened
   - The realization that we were not to blame
     (i.e., we didn't cause what happened)
   - Grieving those ungrieved losses and hurts, and
   - Creating ways to get free from continuing to make
     the same mistakes that result from these unhealed hurts.

If your therapists are trained in using these methods,
they can be done in group and sometimes individual therapy.
If you'd like to try them, tell your therapist.
Family reconstruction takes much longer to do
and is not offered by most therapists.

5. **Hypnosis** and related techniques. These can be helpful if used in the context of a full recovery program. The Ericksonian hypnotic techniques and those that evolve from them are generally the most helpful. Like most of these experiential techniques, if used alone, this will not usually be sufficient for complete healing.

6. **Attending self-help meetings** (see pages 125 to 129).

7. Working the **Twelve Steps** (of ACoA, Al-Anon, AA, NA, OA, etc.) (see page 127).

8. **Group Therapy** — usually a safe place to practice many of these experiential techniques (see page 115).
. . . I have described these above three methods previously.

9. **Couples Therapy** or **Family Therapy**
These can be useful in advanced healing or in specific circumstances. They are generally not useful to heal our Child Within during the first two years or so of our recovery. Family therapy can be damaging when in or outside of the sessions a parent or other family member tries to dominate, control or mistreat an adult child who is in early recovery, since those behaviors tend to compound or repeat the trauma and to force the Child Within back into hiding.

Couples therapy can be helpful if two adult children who are each already active long term in their own recovery program want to work on issues in their relationship.

10. **Guided Imagery** can be helpful when specific for helping us heal our True Self.
Like most of these techniques, it should be used only in the context of a full recovery program.

11. **Breathwork** in the form of either *rebirthing* or *holonomic integration* (holotropic therapy) can supplement a full recovery program. These techniques can be among the more powerful ones in accessing our unconscious mind and should be delivered only by specially trained and experienced therapists. Briefly, holonomic integration is done by lying down in a comfortable place with a guide accompanying each person, and with eyes closed, breathing rapidly while expertly-selected evocative music is played fairly loudly. This experience generally lasts about 1½ to 2 hours, and is often followed by drawing a personal representation of the experience in color and then sharing that drawing and the experience.

This technique can be helpful when a person
- feels "stuck" in their healing process, or
- wants to move a bit faster in their recovery.

Because holonomic integration can be so powerful in helping to
open our unconscious mind and can leave the person
so vulnerable that they feel raw, like an "open wound"
for from a few days to a few weeks afterwards,
I recommend that it be done only if a person is
in ongoing group or individual therapy, and
that it be done not more often than every four to six weeks.

12. Using **Affirmations** can likewise be helpful
when used to supplement a full recovery program.
Like most of these techniques, affirmations are
not as lastingly healing when used alone.
Affirmations help us re-program our old beliefs,
belief systems, thoughts and attitudes about ourself, others
and the universe. In Chapter 25, page 217,
I describe an approach to beginning to change
our negative beliefs.

13. **Dream Analysis** is also helpful in our healing.
Many books and approaches are available.
Our dreams can be a rich source of healing information.
Keep writing materials next to your bed; as you awaken, write
a few words or a few lines to describe your dreams.
For a particularly memorable dream,
i.e., one that tends to stay in your memory longer,
it can be useful to tell that dream to a safe person
and then tell them what you think it could be about.
Dream material comes from our unconscious mind,
and so it tends to be a reflection of what
we might have repressed or "stuffed" and what
our deeper self is perhaps lovingly suggesting that
we consider working through.
But dream language tends to be
in the language of universal symbols
and patterns and of course not in English or a similar language.

So we can become familiar with it by practicing
these above described steps day by day
or whenever we remember any dream.

We can also write out each symbol or image from a dream
and under it "brainstorm" a list of all the
possible meanings and even impossible meanings that
that symbol might have for us in that dream.
It can then be useful to discuss each of these with
a safe person, including our group or therapist.
What might this dream be telling me about
my life and about my recovery?

14. **Art, Movement and Play Therapy** can also
access our unconscious mind.
I have noticed that most artists and people
in the performing arts are adult children
of dysfunctional families. One possibility is that they may be
unconsciously using these arts to help heal themselves,
as are many people in some other professions.

In our therapy, art, movement and play can shift us from our
heads into our hearts and souls and are thus useful
in moving us along in our healing process,
especially if we feel blocked or stuck in any way.

Do you feel blocked or stuck right now in any way?

Would you or your Child Within be interested in getting out
some art materials and seeing what happens if
you let yourself get into them?

Or would you or your Child Within be interested in getting into
some open space and beginning to move around
in *any* way you wish?

Or would you or your Child Within be interested
in playing in *any* way at all, either alone
or with anyone else?

15. **Active Imagination** and **Using Intuition**
These are special techniques described by various therapists
(Johnson 1986, Vaughan 1983). We can learn these
on our own and most Jungian therapists will know
something about using them.
Active Imagination (AI) is an ancient healing method that has
evolved into an effective experiential technique.
It is like dreaming out loud while awake.
AI is a way to help us work through most any conflict.

Its principal method is a dialogue between two opposites in our conflict, like right and wrong, good and evil, masculine and feminine, good and bad or duty and feeling.

The dialogue may be between me and anything with which I may be in conflict. We can use any of a number of methods for this dialogue, such as writing (which Johnson recommends), talking, acting, drawing, painting, sculpting, sand play, role play, family sculpture, dancing or whatever we may create.

AI is "realer than real," hard work,
and then moves us to deep feelings.

To do it, be sure you have at least one hour free in a quiet place. Begin writing whatever comes up for you from
the perspective on one opposite, and then
whatever comes up for the other side of the conflict. Listen without judgment or prejudice to both sides of the dialogue. It is not useful to have one side win, but rather to have a healing, learning and agreement between the two sides of the conflict. Toward the end it is healing to add to the dialogue a moral point of view, involving fairness, rightness or justice.

Then stop writing, etc., and go out into your life
and take whatever appropriate action you may choose to take. Use a therapist or safe friend to talk if you get
stuck or too upset at any time.

Should you try AI, I suggest reading Johnson's book and/or hearing his tape.

Voice dialogue is a related technique that can be used in individual or group therapy or elsewhere (Stone & Winkelman, 1988, 1989).

16. **Meditation and Prayer**, when practiced daily
    and regularly can be powerful balancers and
    integrators of our whole personality and being.
    They can help us realize the *sanity*, the wholeness
    that the Second of the Twelve Steps addresses.
    There are numerous books on meditation and prayer, and
    I discuss these spiritual practices briefly in
    Spirituality in Recovery.
    Both are suggested in the Eleventh Step.

Meditating

One does not have to be at all interested
in religion or even spirituality to learn to meditate effectively. There are several different types of **meditation**.
It is most useful to locate a meditation teacher
and learn from them, while reading a book or two
that they might recommend. If you can't find a teacher and
if you have some free time, you might consider the following.

Find a quiet, comfortable place where you will not
be interrupted for about an hour. It is best not to have eaten for
about two hours and not to have used any psychoactive drugs
or heavy amounts of sugar or sweets for several days.
Drugs, including alcohol, nicotine and caffeine — and sugar —
tend to block a healthy meditation response.

Sit in a comfortable straight-backed chair,
or without the chair, on a pillow or meditation bench.
Whenever you are ready, *begin to quiet your mind*
and to open your heart.

Let your eyes close and take in a deep breath.
Then slowly let the breath out. Repeat several times.

After you have begun to quiet yourself in this way,
say the following two words out loud, clearly —

I AM

Then repeat them in a somewhat softer voice,
and keep repeating *I AM* until it is just a whisper.
Finally, keep repeating it every few seconds,
in your mind only. If distracting thoughts come in,
just watch them as they come and as they go.
There is no need to be in control.
Just begin to let go, and keep repeating the *I AM.*
Somewhere along your way you may notice
a mild altered state of consciousness.
This is usually an indication of beginning healing and
moving toward *Wholeness* or *Sanity.*

This is meditation.

Continue meditating for about 20 minutes,
then when you are ready, slowly open your eyes.
Meditation is safe and it will not interfere
with any recovery, counseling or religion.
In fact, meditation is most likely to **enhance**
and **enrich** all aspects of our psycho-spiritual well-being.
It can have an immediate effect of increased
relaxation and energy. Its longer term effects,
which may take years, include a progressively
increasing awareness of self, others and the universe.
Often serenity and a sense of peace will begin to appear.
It takes regular practice and a lot of patience.

Praying

Similar to meditation, **prayer** can also be healing.
But it takes the same practice and patience.
How do we listen and talk to our Higher Power,
to something that is so mysterious, powerful and pervasive
that we often have difficulty even conceiving of It?
A person can pray at any time, needing no special physical
posture, paraphernalia, house of worship or ceremony.
While it can be helpful to close one's eyes
and take a few slow and deep breaths to get into
a higher state of consciousness to facilitate praying,
even that is not necessary.

What is more important is our "state of heart."

Perhaps the only "requirements" for effective prayer
are faith, surrender or true humility and a loving attitude
to God and our fellow creatures
— states of being which are often difficult to reach.

Christ said (Revelation 3: 20) "Behold, I stand at the door and
knock: if any one hear my voice and open the door,
I will come in to them, and sup with them and they with me."

It is thus not we who move us to pray, but our Higher Power,
perhaps through our Higher Self, which invites us and moves us.
Even if we do not have the above "requirements" for prayer,
we can still pray in any way we choose that will begin
to open ourselves to Universal Consciousness. Whatever
comes — whether it be struggle, resistance or frustration,
or joy and peace — we can experience it. If we continue to
pray with patience and trust, the "required" humility,
love and faith will come.

Prayer and meditation are the breath of the Self,
with each respiration transferring the radiant and healing
energy from Universal Consciousness into us.
When we release ourselves, when we totally relax and
surrender into the radiant energy of our Higher Power,
we begin for the first time to practice with the basic
experience and feeling, as well as the intuitive understanding
that all things and beings are already only direct
manifestation of Universal Consciousness.

We are connected. Our fear and suffering are gone.
We are One.

17. **Therapeutic bodywork** can have many advantages,
    from relaxation to physical well-being to helping us
    get more grounded. There are many techniques,
    including therapeutic massage, Trager, zero balancing,
    Feldenkrais, Reubenfeld and others.

    While useful for all people in helping heal our Child Within,
    these methods can be especially useful for those
    adult children who do not get much physical exercise
    or who may have stored a lot of tension in their body.

    When we were young, many of us were not touched
    enough in a healthy way, and some of us were touched
    in an unhealthy way, such as physical abuse or sexual abuse.

    We may have come to disown parts of our body
    and thus may feel disconnected from it.
    This lack of connection, as well as other factors,
    may have resulted in aches and pains of all sorts.

    Sometimes our unfinished business and conflicts invade
    a part of our body and begin to nag at us.
    Being sure that the physical condition could not be helped
    by a conventional medical approach,
    and depending on the nature of the condition,
    therapeutic bodywork may help.

    Since the Child is a Whole Being,
    including the physical, mental, emotional and spiritual,
    as we heal the mental, emotional and spiritual
    we may sometimes neglect our physical being.
    Of course, the physical is **connected** to the others.
    Through therapeutic bodywork,
    sometimes mental, emotional and spiritual issues arise
    that we discover are important in our healing.

18. **Keeping a journal or a diary** is healing
    for a number of reasons.
    Used in concert with this workbook and guide,
    keeping a journal or diary can strengthen and
    document our healing.

What can I record in my journal or diary? Anything and everything! Including —

- Aspects of my inner life, especially my feelings
- Working through conflicts, including active imagination
- Dreams and my personal dream analysis
- Poetry, sketches or even doodles
- Affirmations that I create
- Memorable quotes
- Questions I might ask myself or others
- Notes from lectures or tapes
- As a scrapbook to tape-in anything —
- Articles, cartoons, pictures
- And more . . .

Use any book with blank pages that feels comfortable. Date each entry for both later reflection and to show your progress.

Write quickly without thinking too much about it.
Just let your hand move and let the words flow across the page.
Challenge yourself with different kinds of expressions,
such as poetry, drawings, crayons, dialogue, etc.

19. **Writing an unmailed letter** to someone with whom you have been in conflict or have any kind of unfinished business can be especially healing.
As do most of these experiential techniques,
writing an unmailed letter *facilitates* the Child Within's

- **Coming out of hiding**
- Expressing its **inner life**
- **Grieving**
- Being **creative**
- **Asserting** itself
- Getting its **needs** met, and
- **Experiencing** its life more fully.

It is important to *process* such an experience
by **sharing** the letter and our feelings about it
with a safe person. Ideally this would be a therapist
and even more healing, a therapy group.
The writer reads the letter to the person or people,
and uses the others as a mirror to get feedback
and to get validation and support. The writer, group and
group leaders may then spontaneously create
other experiential methods of healing as are appropriate.

Following are some questions to consider when considering
and deciding to whom you may write an unmailed letter.

- With whom in your life do you have any important
  unfinished business?

- With whom do you have one or more important **conflicts**
  that you would **like to heal**?

- Who has **mistreated** you or **abused** you?

- Whom might *you* have hurt, mistreated or abused?

- About whom might you be carrying a **resentment**?

The main goals of the letter are to express yourself more fully
and to begin to release toxic painful feelings.

The person to whom you write may be living or not,
any age and any relationship to you at all.
Take as much time as you need to think about
this possibility in writing the letter and
in working through any of your conflicts or issues with them.

Nearly always there will be some healing without mailing
the letter. Should you ever contemplate *mailing* such a letter,
I suggest that you ask your therapy group, therapist,
or best friend for feedback on this question.

Can you think of *any possible* person or people
that you would like to write such a letter?

On the next page are some spaces in which to write the names
of any possible people and any issues or
conflicts you might even remotely have.

Use extra paper for more names and issues.

From any of your listed people (places or things), to whom
might you want to write the first letter? Place a 1 by their name.
And a 2, and so on, for the next ones.

When you are ready, should you decide,
use a separate piece of paper to write the letter.
Then read it to a safe person and/or to your therapy group.

Chart 18.1. Unfinished Business

Person's Name	Conflicts or Issues

It is usually best *not* to read such a letter to a Twelve-Step self-help group. When you have completed the letter, store it in a safe place since it is so personal and private.

What was it like to write and talk about the above?
Use the space below for your reflections.

20. Using a **workbook** like this one.
    There are several workbooks available
    for healing, growth and wellness.
    They use various approaches and exercises,
    and each takes points of view that differ
    somewhat to a lot. Each of these may be
    used on any of several levels, which I discuss
    on pages 146 through 150.

To *get the most* from this book, I have suggested that a person

- Read it

- Work through the exercises slowly,
  at their own pace, and concomitantly

- Work a full recovery program.

Using this book in this way, according to our own individual needs,
our healing will usually gradually unfold
over a span of from at least three to five years.

And it is perfectly fine if it continues for
a longer period — again based on our individual needs.

While we may at times feel impatient and in a hurry
to get free of our pain, confusion and whatever else
we may want to let go, healing our Child Within
is most completely done when it is *not rushed.*
The Child Itself knows when and at what pace to proceed.

21. **Creating** our **own** experiential **techniques** or healing.
    Here I have free rein to create whatever
    might be healing for me.
    I have seen people use old photos in all sorts of ways,
    do drawings or other art work, make tape recordings,
    create personal affirmations, write and sing songs,
    write poetry and stories — the list is endless —
    Any ideas?
    Let flow whatever may come up for you at any time.

    There is a lot of material in this chapter.
    As you work through any of it,
    be sure to take a break frequently.

Some Cautions

Like most things in our life, experiential techniques
can have a "double-edged sword" quality. They can have
advantages and disadvantages. While they usually help us
in our healing, at times they can block our healing.
Throughout this book I have described some of their uses
and cautions and will now summarize three potential blocks.

Traps in Using Experiential Techniques

- **Addiction to their "quick hit," "fix" or "rush"** — Some of
the more dramatic or fast-acting experiential techniques can
open us to our deep feelings and other parts of our inner life so
quickly or effectively that we believe they are the only way that
we can open up. Like an addiction, we think there is no other
way. This can limit our ability to open up to ourself and our
feelings spontaneously and in a number of other healthy ways.

- **Diversion from living life authentically** — Focused so much
on the technique, we can thus become diverted from living our
life naturally, from, through and as our True Self.

- **Excluding less dramatic techniques** that are equally or
even more healing — Some experiential techniques are less
dramatic and more subtle, and their healing works more slowly.
For example, just being real, speaking from our heart, can be
just as healing as the most dramatic, action-oriented family
sculpture.

As I heal my Child Within, I can use experiential techniques
constructively, while being aware if I were to become
overly attached to their trappings and their drama.

If anything is coming up for you now around any of the above,
or if anything comes up later, use the space below and on the next
page to write about it.

<u>Notes</u>

If working through any of this material in any part of this book gets to be too painful or confusing for you, I suggest that you contact a professional therapist for a consultation (see page 130), and that you slow down on your use of this material.

19

Setting Boundaries
And Limits

As a child, when we were mistreated or abused,
our Child Within protected itself by going into hiding,
often deep within the unconscious part of itself (see also page 28).

As I recover and heal, I discover that my True Self
needs to go into hiding less and less.
I gradually learn that the safest person with whom
I can let free — and be — my Child Within is *myself.*
The next are safe others, fellow travelers in my recovery process.
Also sponsors, counselors and therapists.
And best friends and trusted others.
I learn that with these people my Child Within can come out
and stay out, as long as It continues to feel accepted and safe.

But at certain times, even with these safe people —
and surely often with unsafe people — my Child Within
may not want to go into hiding. This is because I feel
more aware, powerful and creative when It is conscious and alive.

Since I know that recovery includes sensing
and seeing progressively
more *possibilities* and potential *choices* in my life,
and then making healthy choices,
I begin to see that setting boundaries and limits
can be a healthy choice.
This is because the boundary or limit can protect the safety
and integrity of my Child Within so that It can remain out,
alive and aware, and not always have to go into hiding.

I can begin to define a boundary or limit as
how far I or another can go in a relationship with comfort.
A boundary is a concept that provokes a real experience within us.
Therefore, in my relationship with people, places and things,
the boundary is real. My boundaries and limits are real.
The other's boundaries and limits are real.

Having an awareness of boundaries and limits first helps us
discover who we are.
Until I know who I am, it will be difficult
for me to have healthy relationships, whether they may be
casual acquaintances, friends, close relationships
or intimate relationships.

And at the opposite end of the relationship spectrum,
without an awareness of boundaries, it will be difficult for me
to sort out who is unsafe to be around, which may include people
who are toxic for me, and even some people
who may mistreat or abuse me.

Checking My Boundaries

How can I begin to know what my boundaries and limits are?
I may have grown up in a family where healthy boundaries
were neither modeled nor taught.
And I may have been — and may still be —
in one or more relationships
where I and others are unclear about boundaries and limits.
The following is a survey wherein anyone interested can check
out their own personal boundaries and limits.

Survey On Personal Boundaries

Circle or check the word that most applies to how you truly feel.

1. I can't make up my mind.

   Never   Seldom   Occasionally   Often   Usually

2. I have difficulty saying "no" to people.

   Never   Seldom   Occasionally   Often   Usually

3. I feel like my happiness depends on other people.

   Never   Seldom   Occasionally   Often   Usually

4. It's hard for me to look a person in the eyes.

   Never   Seldom   Occasionally   Often   Usually

5. I find myself getting involved with people who end up hurting me.

   Never   Seldom   Occasionally   Often   Usually

6. I trust others.

   Never   Seldom   Occasionally   Often   Usually

7. I would rather attend to others than attend to myself.

   Never   Seldom   Occasionally   Often   Usually

8. Others' opinions are more important than mine.

   Never   Seldom   Occasionally   Often   Usually

9. People take or use my things without asking me.

   Never   Seldom   Occasionally   Often   Usually

10. I have difficulty asking for what I want or what I need.

    Never   Seldom   Occasionally   Often   Usually

11. I lend people money and don't seem to get it back on time.

    Never   Seldom   Occasionally   Often   Usually

12. Some people who I lend money don't ever pay me back.

    Never   Seldom   Occasionally   Often   Usually

13. I feel ashamed.

    Never   Seldom   Occasionally   Often   Usually

14. I would rather go along with another person or other people than express what I'd really like to do.

Never   Seldom   Occasionally   Often   Usually

15. I feel bad for being so "different" from other people.

Never   Seldom   Occasionally   Often   Usually

16. I feel fear, anxious, scared, or afraid.

Never   Seldom   Occasionally   Often   Usually

17. I spend my time and energy helping others so much that I neglect my own wants and needs.

Never   Seldom   Occasionally   Often   Usually

18. It's hard for me to know what I believe and what I think.

Never   Seldom   Occasionally   Often   Usually

19. I feel like my happiness depends on circumstances outside of me.

Never   Seldom   Occasionally   Often   Usually

20. I feel good.

Never   Seldom   Occasionally   Often   Usually

21. I have a hard time knowing what I really feel.

Never   Seldom   Occasionally   Often   Usually

22. I find myself getting involved with people who end up being bad for me.

Never   Seldom   Occasionally   Often   Usually

23. It's hard for me to make decisions.

Never   Seldom   Occasionally   Often   Usually

24. I get angry.

Never   Seldom   Occasionally   Often   Usually

25. I don't get to spend much time alone.

Never   Seldom   Occasionally   Often   Usually

26. I tend to take on the moods of people close to me.

Never   Seldom   Occasionally   Often   Usually

27. I have a hard time keeping a confidence or secret.

Never   Seldom   Occasionally   Often   Usually

28. I am overly sensitive to criticism.

    Never   Seldom   Occasionally   Often   Usually

29. I feel hurt.

    Never   Seldom   Occasionally   Often   Usually

30. I tend to stay in relationships that are hurting me.

    Never   Seldom   Occasionally   Often   Usually

31. I feel an emptiness, like something is missing in my life.

    Never   Seldom   Occasionally   Often   Usually

32. I tend to get caught up "in the middle" of other people's problems.

    Never   Seldom   Occasionally   Often   Usually

33. When someone I'm with acts up in public, I tend to feel embarrassed.

    Never   Seldom   Occasionally   Often   Usually

34. I feel sad.

    Never   Seldom   Occasionally   Often   Usually

35. It's not easy for me to really know in my heart about my relationship with a Higher Power or God.

    Never   Seldom   Occasionally   Often   Usually

36. I prefer to rely on what others say about what I should believe and do about religious or spiritual matters.

    Never   Seldom   Occasionally   Often   Usually

37. I tend to take on or feel what others are feeling.

    Never   Seldom   Occasionally   Often   Usually

38. I put more into relationships than I get out of them.

    Never   Seldom   Occasionally   Often   Usually

39. I feel responsible for other people's feelings.

    Never   Seldom   Occasionally   Often   Usually

40. My friends or acquaintances have a hard time keeping secrets or confidences which I tell them.

    Never   Seldom   Occasionally   Often   Usually

Assessing and Scoring This Survey

Assessing and scoring this survey is similar to that of
the *Recovery Potential Survey* on Page 12.
The more "Usuallys" and "Oftens" tend to indicate
more boundary issues.
They may also indicate some confusion over boundaries and limits,
often called "blurred" boundaries. A person who answered
all or mostly "Nevers" may not be aware of their boundaries.
A person who has healed their Child Within would tend to answer
many "Seldoms" and some "Occasionallys."
Rare items, like number 20, would be scored in the reverse.
If you have any questions about any of these areas and
dimensions of boundaries and limits, ask your therapist,
counselor, therapy group or other appropriate person
— including your own Child Within. (I describe this scoring
in more detail in my book on Boundaries.)

It may be helpful now to begin to summarize areas
in which you may have some boundary issues or problems.
To do so, refer to your answers from the *Survey.*
Underline or circle the key words or phrases to which you answered
"Usually," "Often" and "Never." (While some "Nevers" may not
indicate a boundary issue for you, many will.
Ask for feedback from safe people if you are uncertain.)
Also consider *other areas* in your life that are *not*
included in the *Survey,* in which you may have now or in the past
had any possible concern about your personal boundaries.

Below is some space in which to summarize these.

Boundaries or limits can be subdivided into being important in the
physical, mental-emotional and spiritual areas of our life.
Based on all of the above, below are some spaces in which
to summarize any aspect of your life where boundaries
may be an issue.

Physical Boundary Problems or Issues

Mental and Emotional Boundary Problems or Issues

Spiritual Boundary Problems or Issues

As any of these may come up for you in your life,
consider discussing them with selected safe people,
such as your therapist, counselor, therapy group, sponsor or best
friend.
It may also be helpful to write about what comes up for you
in your diary or journal. Remember to protect your boundaries
by keeping what you write in a safe place.

Some More About Boundaries

The boundary marks or delineates the differences between me
and the other. Without boundaries, it would be hard to define myself.
Without boundaries, I may not feel that I *have* a self.
And without boundaries, I can't have a healthy self.
So, by being aware of and having boundaries, I can better define
and know myself, know that I have a self,
and have a healthy self.

A key to my boundaries is *knowing my inner life*.
My inner life includes my beliefs, thoughts, feelings,
choices, decisions, wants, needs, sensations within my body,
my intuitions, and even unconscious factors in my life.
If I am unaware of or out of tune with my inner life,
I can't know all of my boundaries and limits.
When I am aware of my inner life,
I can more readily know my boundaries.

The co-dependent person tends to be fixed in either few
or no boundaries — boundarilessness — or the opposite:
overly rigid boundaries.
And they often flip-flop between these.
Because they focus so much of their attention outside of themself,
they tend to be less aware of their inner life,
and thus less aware of their boundaries.

Without knowing my inner life and my boundaries,
I am unable to know my True Self, my Child Within,
and I am unable to protect its well-being and its integrity.

Another key to having healthy boundaries is flexibility and adaptability.
When I am able to be flexible and adaptable in a relationship — without being mistreated or abused — I can know myself in a deeper and richer way.
And I can more easily let go enough into the experience of that relationship to enjoy both its fun aspects and its growth points.

Healthy Boundaries

Healthy boundaries and limits are necessary in —

- **Self-definition** and self **care**
- All aspects of **healing** my Child Within
    - — Being real
    - — Identifying and getting my needs met
    - — Grieving my ungrieved losses and hurts
    - — Working through my core issues and basic dynamics
- **Healthy relationships**
  Boundaries protect my Child Within's reality
- Realizing **Serenity**
  With healthy boundaries, I can then let go and live in healthy relationship with self, others and Higher Power.

But how can I know when my boundaries and limits are **healthy?** Some possible criteria follow:

1. **Presence** — To have boundary health — the usefulness or non-usefulness of a boundary — a boundary has to be present in my awareness.

2. **Appropriateness, based on my inner life** — This begins to delineate some *useful reasons why* I may need the boundary.

3. **Protective** — The boundary is useful to help protect the well-being and integrity of my Child Within.

4. **Firmness** — To get what I want or need, how *firm* do I want my boundary or limit to be?

5. **Maintenance** — Do I need to hold firm on a specific boundary or limit for a period of time, to get what my Child Within wants or needs? Or do I need to *relax* the boundary or limit to get what my Child Within wants or needs?

6. **Flexibility** — To get what I want or need, how *flexible* do I want my boundary or limit to be?

7. **Receptive** — Would it be useful or enjoyable for me to loosen the boundary a bit and let another in?

> **My boundaries and limits protect the well-being and integrity of my Child Within.**

I discuss boundaries and limits in more detail in my audiotaped talk on them, available as a single tape or as part of an album (volume 3 of my Core Issues series) available from ACCESS. I also describe and expand them, with several case history examples and some exercises, in a new book, *Boundaries and Limits in Relationships and Recovery* (working title for 1991).

20

Visiting My Family Of Origin

. . . And The Usefulness Of Age Regression

It can be painful to visit our family of origin.
And depending on our and their healing, it can be joyful.

Our family of origin is whoever we grew up with.
For some it is our mother, father and siblings.
For others it is mostly a single parent, or perhaps
a step-parent, with step-brothers and step-sisters.
Or it could be foster parents. Or one or more
grandparents could have helped raise us.

Others could live in the house — uncles,
aunts, cousins, in-laws, even "boarders,"
and any of these could change at any time,
and they could change often.
And our geographic location could change.
But whoever was there, and whenever it was,
and wherever some of those people might be now,
we often have some people and a place that we visit.
It may feel like we are drawn to them,
like a magnet or like some kind of roots
that we put down, and now we must return ever so often.
We may even call it "home" — even when we don't live there.

A question is —

"Why return?"

There could be any number
of reasons why we may return, such as —

- To enjoy spending time with them
- To share with them
- To please them
- To try to get their approval or acceptance
- To fulfill an obligation
- To prove something to them
- To *attempt* to prove something to them
- To prove something to myself
- To fix them
- To fix myself
- To heal a hurt or a difference
- For the children
- For religious purposes
- To be part of a special occasion,
  such as a birthday or a holiday
- To get something
- To borrow something
- To borrow money — or any reason at all —

_____

_____
(fill in the blanks)

There is nothing wrong with going to visit
our family of origin for any of these reasons.
However, a problem can develop when we visit
and we are **unaware** of **why** we are going.

Having a decreased awareness of any of these above reasons can set ourself up for unnecessary pain and suffering.

Would your Child Within be interested —
the next time you visit any of these people —
to know why it is going to visit?
Or why co-dependent self is going to visit?

What would be useful for it to know about such a visit?

We can begin to consider some of the following questions.
    (If you'd like, write your answers or reflections
        next to and below each question.)

Who am I going to visit?

Why?

What has been my past experience when I visited them?

What happened during the visit?

Did any of it remind me of any parts of my childhood?

Or remind me of any other part of my past?

What were my feelings then?

What is likely to happen this time?

What feelings might I be likely to have?

Who am I taking with me?

How safe are they?

How safe are the people I am going to visit?

What are my expectations for this visit?

Is there something I would rather do than this visit?

What would I rather do?

Do I need to protect my Child Within?

How can I protect my Child Within?

What can I learn from this visit?

After you make this visit, consider the following.

What did I observe during this visit?

How was I different?

Was I more **aware** than I was in the past?

What happened?

How was my Child Within?

Knowing the above, is there anything that I would do any differently now?

Did I share any of the above experiences with anyone? Who?

Were they safe?

What was their response or feedback?

Did I share any of this with my therapy group, therapist, sponsor, best friend or the like?

What was their reaction and feedback?

How is my Child Within right now?

Do I feel like my Child Within is healing?

How do I know?

Take some time and reflect on your experiences while making this visit and any sharing that you might have done around or after the visit. If you'd like, write your reactions or reflections below.

After your visit(s), and after answering some of these questions, you might now be able to revise some of what you began writing in Chapters 5, 6, 7, 8, 12 and 13. Take as much time as you need in making any revisions, additions or subtractions in any of these chapters.

What was it like for you to do these exercises?

A common occurrence from which we can learn and grow when we visit our family of origin is age regression.

Age Regression

Just **learning** about age regression can be healing.
Age regression happens when we suddenly feel upset,
confused and scared, like a helpless young little child.
There may be no apparent cause for it,
and it may last a few minutes or longer.
It can feel as though one minute we are an adult
feeling okay, and in a matter of seconds
we feel like an out-of-control and helpless little person.

Has anything like that ever happened to you?

We can begin to heal ourselves around such an
age regression when one happens by beginning to **observe**
our **inner life** and what is happening **around** us.

As we heal our Child Within, we can discover
that age regression is actually a healing gift in disguise.

There is usually a **trigger** that initiates the
rapid sequence of age regression. This trigger
may be any of number of possibilities, including —

- Any **mistreatment** or **abandonment** by anyone
  (e.g., see Table 7.1 on page 53)

- Any **negative message** from anyone (e.g., see page 57)

- Any form of **invalidation**

- Anything that *reminds* us of any of the above.

We can age regress at any time, in any place,
for any reason. Immediately after the triggering event,
we may suddenly feel the following in rapid sequence

- Fear
- Hurt
- Shame
- Guilt
- Anger
- Confusion
- Disorientation

. . . And end up feeling dysfunctional and out of control,
almost like we want to scream. But our Child feels too weak
even for that, so it may want just to go into hiding.

When age regression continues to wound us repeatedly,
with no healing around it, we may remain paralyzed,
confused and dysfunctional and our Child Within stays in hiding.

When we recognize it and heal it, age regression
can be a great factor in our healing and well-being.

Healing Age Regression

1. The first step in healing age regression is to **recognize** it
   when it happens. This is a kind of **self-diagnosis**.
   Visiting our family of origin is often an opportune time
   to self-diagnose age regression
   because we tend to get mistreated,
   mentally or emotionally abandoned,
   or invalidated there so frequently.

   When it happens, I might say to myself something like,
   "Hey, I'm age regressing now," or "I just age regressed."

   This is a great moment because when we **name it**,
   we can do something about it.

2. We can then begin to take some slow, **deep breaths**.

3. And then begin to **walk around** the room.
   The point is not to be immobilized, since that may contribute
   to perpetuating our feeling of immobilization and helplessness.
   And then begin to **look** at various objects in the room.
   Walk into another room and do the same.

4. Get a hold of our **keys** and begin to play with them.
   Keys are symbolic of freedom. They open doors
   and start car engines. An accompanying practice
   in preventing and managing the sometimes crippling effects
   of age regression is, when convenient, **always have a way out**
   of our family member's house for when the going gets too difficult.
   We can bring our car, stay in a motel or have
   some other way to get out should we need to.

5. As soon as possible **talk about it** with a **safe** person.
   This is why when convenient it can be helpful to bring
   a safe person with us when we visit. If there is no one
   to talk with, we can write down what happened and how it felt
   and then talk it over with a safe person later.

6. Later we can **talk** about it **some more**.
   This is a great healing opportunity, and it can be
   most helpful to talk it over with our therapy group,
   therapist or other safe person or people.

7. It is helpful eventually to **work through** what happened and how it felt during the age regression in an **experiential** way. Some techniques to facilitate this include —

- Telling our story
- Anger bat work
- Writing and reading (to a safe person) an unmailed letter
- Family sculpture
- Gestalt techniques
- Any creative technique

8. Consider the **levels of meaning** the age regression may have for us. For example —

Level 1 — I was mistreated in the past.
     2 — I am being mistreated now.
     3 — I don't want to be mistreated anymore.
     4 — I'm going to set firm limits in this relationship.
     5 — I'm going to leave this relationship if the mistreatment continues.
     6 — I can get free of this unnecessary pain and suffering.
     7 — I am learning and growing from this age regression.
     8 — By using it, I am healing my Child Within.

9. **Recognize** these **triggers** and other triggering events *as they come up* for us. By doing so, we can then avoid situations where we may anticipate that they will happen.

10. **Use** all of the above **constructively**.
For example,
- recognize and heal any future age regressions,
- avoid people who do triggering behaviors,
- protect our Child Within,
- stop blaming ourself, and
- bring the unconscious in our life more into our full awareness.

Thus handled, age regressions can be healing for us since they get us in touch with our past unhealed injuries. We heal ourselves in this way in a safe environment. If we are *continually* exposed to mistreatment, we can heal an age regression in a safe place, like our therapy group, etc.

Age regressions may be associated with panic attacks, and the above steps can be helpful in some panic attacks.

Age regression is a sudden decompensation that is triggered by a hurt. It occurs commonly among adult children of unhealthy families and in people with post-traumatic stress disorder.

Use the following chart to write about any age regressions.

Chart 20.1. Age Regressions

Triggering Event	What Came Up For Me	How I Handled It	Its Meaning For Me

Chart 20.1. (cont'd)

Triggering Event	What Came Up For Me	How I Handled It	Its Meaning For Me

If one or more of our family members are not safe for us,
we can choose *not* to visit them anymore or to visit them less often,
or to limit or modify any time we might spend with them.
We can **choose** to **set** any boundaries and **limits** that might be
most healing for our Child Within.

What are your reactions to these statements?
And to this chapter?

Write them in the space below.

21

Risking, Sharing
And
Telling My Story

To heal, we become progressively aware of
and share our vulnerable Child Within with ourself
with safe others and if we choose,
with our Higher Power.

But risking, sharing and telling our real story
may not come easy.

In preparing for some experiential exercises
in risking and telling our story
I reprint three pages from *HCW* (Chapter 12).

Risking

When we risk, we expose our*self,* our Child Within, our True Self. We take a chance and we become vulnerable. When we do this, two extreme outcomes may emerge — acceptance or rejection. Whatever we may decide to risk about ourself, another may accept, reject — or they may react somewhere in between.

Many of us may have been so wounded from risking — whether in our childhood, adolescence, adulthood or all three — that we are usually reluctant or unable to risk and share our Real Self with others. Yet we are caught in a dilemma: when we hold in our feelings, thoughts, concerns and creativities, our Child Within becomes stifled and we feel bad, we hurt. Our held-in energy may build up so much that the only way we can handle it is to let it out to *someone.* This is the predicament that many of us who grew up in troubled families encounter. And because of a number of factors, such as our seeking approval, validation, excitement and intimacy, we may select someone who is *not safe* and supportive. Indeed, they may reject us or betray us in some way, which may just confirm our reluctance to risk. So we hold in all our feelings again and the cycle continues. Yet to heal our Child Within we have to share it with others. So where do we start?

Rather than hold it in and then let it out impulsively or haphazardly, we can begin a step at a time. Find someone who we know is safe and supportive, such as a trusted friend, a counselor or therapist, a therapy group or a sponsor. Begin by risking one little thing. Follow the share-check-share guideline described above (Gravitz, Bowden, 1985). If it works, share some more.

Risking and sharing involves several other core issues, including trust, control, feelings, fear of abandonment, all-or-none thinking and behaving, and high tolerance for inappropriate behavior. When any of these issues come up, it can be useful to consider and even to begin talking about it with safe people.

As we risk, we can eventually begin to tell our story.

Telling Our Story

Telling our story is a powerful act in discovering and healing our Child Within. It is a foundation of recovery in self-help groups, group therapy and individual psychotherapy and counseling. I describe some of the dynamics of story telling in *Spirituality in Recovery.*

Each of our stories when complete contains three basic parts: separation, initiation and return (Campbell, 1988). Twelve-Step self-help groups describe their stories as "What we were like," "What happened" and "What we are like now." People in group therapy may call it risking, sharing, participating and "working" in group. In individual counseling or psychotherapy we may describe it by similar names, and psychoanalysts may call it "free association, working through transference and through unsolved internal conflict." Among close friends, we may call it "baring our souls" or "having a heart-to-heart talk."

In sharing and telling our story we can be aware that gossip and wallowing in our pain are usually counterproductive to healing. This is in part because gossip tends to be attacking rather than self-disclosing and it is generally incomplete, following the victim stance or cycle. Wallowing in our pain is continuing to express our suffering beyond a reasonable duration for healthy grieving. There is a danger here that may be observed in some self-help meetings: When a person tries to tell a painful story that has no apparent or immediate resolution, the other members may unknowingly label it as "self-pity" or a "pity party." In this case, while self-help meetings are generally safe and supportive, the bereaved may wish to look elsewhere to express their pain.

Simos (1979) said, "Grief work must be shared. In sharing, however, there must be no impatience, censure or boredom with the repetition, because repetition is necessary for catharsis and internalization and eventual unconscious acceptance of the reality of the loss. The bereaved are sensitive to the feelings of others and will not only refrain from revealing feelings to those they consider unequal to the burden of sharing the grief but may even try to comfort the helpers" (*i.e.,* the listener).

Our story does not have to be a classical "drunkalog" or long in length. In telling our story we talk about what is important, meaningful, confusing, conflicting or painful in our life. We risk, share, interact, discover and more. And by so doing we heal ourselves. While we can listen to the stories of others, and they can listen to ours, perhaps the most healing feature is that *we,* the story teller, *get to hear our own story.* While we may have an idea about what our story is whenever we tell it, it usually comes out different from what we initially thought.

I have illustrated our story in Figure 21.1. Starting at the point on the circle called "contentment," we can forget that we are *in* our story. Eventually in our day-to-day life we experience a loss, whether it be a real or a threatened loss. The stage is now set for both grieving and growing. In Figure 21.1 I have summarized most of the initial pain of our grieving as *hurt.* And when we feel hurt, we tend to get angry.

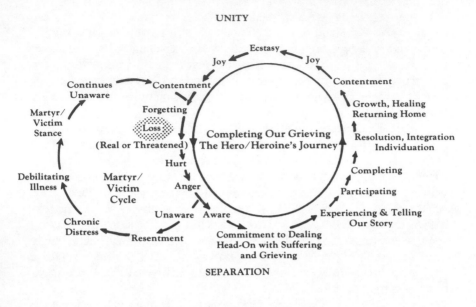

UNITY

SEPARATION

Figure 21.1. OUR STORY

At this crucial point we have a *possibility* of becoming *aware* that we have experienced a loss or are suffering an upset. And here we can choose to make a *commitment to facing our suffering and grieving head-on.* We can call this cycle of our story a "completed" one or the "hero/heroine's journey." *Or* we may remain *unaware* of the possibility of working through our suffering around our loss or upset. We may then begin to build up a resentment and/or to blame ourselves, which eventually leads to stress-related illness, and to more prolonged suffering than if we had worked through our upset and our grieving in the first place. We can call this cycle the "victim cycle" or the "martyr/victim stance."

If we commit to work through our pain and grieving, we then begin to share, ventilate, participate and to experience our suffering. We may need to tell our story in such a fashion several times periodically over a period of several hours, days, weeks or even months — in order to finally complete our story. We may also have to consider it in other ways, mull it over, dream about it and even tell it again.

While this has been painful for us, we are now complete with our upset or conflict. We are free of its pain. Our conflict is now resolved and integrated. We have learned from it. We have healed our Child Within and have grown. And we can settle back to our natural state of our Child Within, which is contentment, joy and creativity.

However, to begin to tell our story may be difficult. And when we tell it, it may be difficult to express our feelings around it.

To start this exercise, begin to think about which parts of your story you have told, to whom you have told these parts and about how much telling them assisted you in experiencing your Child Within.

Use the space below to write anything that comes up for you.

Chart 21.1. My Story

Which Parts of My Story I Have Told	To Whom, When and Where	How Telling Them Assisted Me in Exploring and Knowing My Child Within

Reflecting back on your life and on what you've read
and worked through so far in this book,
is there anything that you may not have told a safe person
that it might be healing for you to tell?
Take as long as you need to reflect and whenever you like,
write anything that may come up for you in the space below.

After you have written some aspects or experiences of your life,
think about to whom it might be safe to tell these.
Remember that there is no rush to tell anyone,
although it will likely be healing to talk to a safe person
or persons about these aspects or experiences of your life.
When you tell them, ask for *what you want* from them
as they listen. Use the checklist of possibilities from page 68.
To help sort out your story and your telling it,
you can use the following outline to make some notes.

Chart 21.2. Telling My Story

What I'd Like To Tell	To Whom	What I'd Like From Them

When you tell your story or work on any issue, it is useful to . . .

- Stay as focused as possible.

- Avoid getting off on side tracks or issues.

- Speak from your True Self.

- Use "I" messages, i.e., when speaking of yourself keep it in the first person. Don't use "you" when you mean "I".

- Express and describe as many related aspects of your inner life as possible, especially feelings.

- Stay in the here and now as much as possible

It is useful to plan what you want to work on or tell,
but you don't need to rehearse exactly
how and what you will say.
However, writing down what you might say can be helpful.

Our story is ongoing. It evolves and continues
as we get to know and heal our Child Within.

As we recover, we gradually shift our story
from that of being a martyr-victim to being a Hero/Heroine.
These are described in *HCW* on pages 110-112
and all of its Chapter 14.

As we complete one story, we then move on to create
and co-create a new and bigger story, one that is closer
to the Truth of our True Self, in its divinely mysterious connection to
the Universe, Higher Power or God/Goddess/All That Is.

In this sense, our story is really a "never-ending story."

You can use the next page to write about
any aspects of your story that might come up for you.

Would you like to take a break now?

Notes

22

Grieving

No matter what age we may be,
when we experience a loss, hurt or trauma,
our Child Within needs three things
to grieve them to a healthy completion —

1. Skills about how to do the grief work,

2. Safe and supportive others, and

3. Enough time to complete the process.

But growing up in a troubled or unhealthy family
may not have allowed us these critical components
of healthy grieving.
In fact, we may have received the opposite.

When we experience a loss, hurt or trauma, it stirs up
energy within us that needs to be discharged.
When we do not discharge this energy, the stress
builds up to a state of chronic distress that we carry inside
wherever we go. This ungrieved grief or chronic distress
can appear as many of the manifestations of being an adult child.

Unresolved grief festers like a deep wound covered by scar tissue,
a pocket of vulnerability ever ready to break out anew.
It stifles our aliveness, creativity and serenity.

Growing up — and even persisting into our adulthood —
we adult children suffered many losses, hurts and traumas
that we never got to grieve to completion.
Now, as we heal our Child Within and recover,
we grieve these formerly ungrieved losses to a healthy completion.
But how can we do that? First, let's look at
some of the rules or guidelines that we *might have been taught*
about how to handle a loss, hurt or trauma.
As I describe these, consider whether you might
have been taught any of them.

Rules We Learned For (Unhealthy) Grieving

(modified from James and others)

- **Don't feel.** It really doesn't hurt. And if it does
  it's not really so bad. Don't talk about your feelings.
  In summary, "stuff your pain."

- **Replace the loss immediately.** Replace it with any person,
  place, thing, behavior, experience or activity that will fill
  the emptiness and take away the pain.

- **Time will heal the loss.** All you really need is enough
  time. And by the way, don't take too long, because things
  are never really as bad as they seem.

- **Don't talk about the loss.** It makes others uncomfortable
  and they don't want to see you uncomfortable either.

- **Change the subject.** If pain and grief come up,
  talk about something else, such as the weather
  or something pleasant or at least neutral.

- **Grieve alone.** There's no reason to make others unhappy
  if you have to be. So don't let anyone see
  or hear you being in pain or upset.

- **Watch how I handle a loss.** Parents, older siblings,
  and similar people usually model for us
  several or even all of the above
  unhealthy ways of handling a loss, hurt or trauma.

It is no surprise, then, that we never learned
how to grieve in a healthy way.
Not only did no one teach us or model healthy grieving for us,
we were taught the *opposite* — how *not* to grieve.
And so we may have stored up a lot of ungrieved grief.

As we begin to grieve and heal our Child Within,
we can think back and remember little things and big things
that happened to us — any losses, hurts or traumas.
In doing so, we can joggle our memory by making
a historical graph based on our age or on the year of the loss.
Use the next page on the right to construct your graph.

Start by writing the year you were born on the far left side
of the page, and then write the year and/or your age on the far right.
Below the year or age of each write any losses, hurts or traumas
that you can even remotely remember.
Although you can start at any time, you might begin as far back
as you can remember. Above the time line on the graph,
indicate any important new events or relationships
you might have experienced, some or parts of which
you might have lost or by which you might have been hurt.

Then write how you were influenced or taught
to handle the grief of each, and then how you actually handled it.

Finally write any important events in your healing or
your recovery from any condition whatsoever.

On the next page is an example Loss History, and on page 200 is
a list of examples of loss from Chapter 11 of *HCW.*
It might be helpful to read or re-read that chapter
sometime during your healing process.

Chart 22.1. My Loss History

	Before / then	Age 4	5½	13	15	16	22	24	34	46	47	48	49
Important New Events or Relationships		Now live with Grandmother and Step Grandfather, Life secure & consistent for the first time.	Re-establish rel'n with family		First "Love" Several healthy and unhealthy role models		College	Professional School Married			Several relationships		My age or year now
My Age, or Year													
Description of Loss, Hurt or Trauma	Beginning of loss of my Child Within. Never had healthy parenting.	Father abandons Mother, sister and me. Mother abandons me by shipping me to a distant city.	Return to parents. Loss of grandmother, etc., above, and school and friends and being center of attention.	Shipped to boarding school as family scapegoat. Loss of family, school, friends and more self-esteem.		Lost her when she married suddenly.	Further loss of True Self Lost spirit became atheist		Divorced. Loss of wife and daughter Several relationships lost	Lost job			Serious medical illness Lost rel'n
How I was Influenced to Handle the Grief	No healthy role models taught, mostly unhealthy rules for grieving (see p. 196.)						Many more unhealthy role models				Saw first healthy role model		
How I Handled My Grief		Stuffed it. Acted like a "big boy" or a "man", or ignored my pain as best I could	I never go to grieve any of this. I mostly stuffed it all.				Retreated into sports, intellect & profession				First time to grieve a loss to a healthy completion Continued healthy grieving		
Important Events in My Healing and Recovery								Marriage counseling	Began spiritual quest and meditation; began ACoDF recovery AC self-help				Psychotherapy Healthy rel'n

Chart 22.2. My Loss History

Important New Events or Relationships	My Age, or Year	Description of Loss, Hurt or Trauma	How I was Influenced to Handle the Grief	How I Handled My Grief	Important Events in My Healing and Recovery

This may be a big project to undertake, so take
as much time as you may need. And you can
return to add to your Loss History as often as you wish.

Below is a list of some common losses that people experience.
Reviewing these may assist you in making your Loss History.

TABLE 22.1. Some Examples of Loss (Compiled from Simos, 1979)

Important Person — Close or Meaningful Relationships
> Separation, divorce, rejection, desertion, abandonment, death, abortion,
> stillbirth, illness, geographic move, children leaving home, etc.

Part of Ourself
> Body image, illness, accident, loss of function, loss of control, self-
> esteem, independence, ego, expectations, lifestyle; needs; culture-
> shock; job, etc., change.

Childhood
> Healthy parenting, getting needs met, healthy development (through
> stages), transitional objects (blanket, soft toy, etc.), gain *or* loss of
> siblings or other family members, body changes (*e.g.,* in adolescence,
> middle age and older age). Threats of loss; separation or divorce.

Adult Developmental
> Transitions, including mid-life.

External Objects
> Money, property, necessities (keys, wallet, etc.), car, sentimental objects,
> collections.

When you have completed as much as you can
    or as much as you have time for, take a break,
        before going on to the next section.

Looking back now at your Loss History,
    which losses, hurts or traumas
        do you sense that you have really completed in your grief work?

And which do you feel like you have not completed?
    Write your answers in the space on the next page.

Also include what you sense has been blocking your grieving
    of these ungrieved losses, hurts, or traumas.

Finally write your plan to complete your work of grieving.

Chart 22.3. My Grieving

My Ungrieved Losses, Hurts or Traumas	What Has Been Blocking My Grieving	How I Plan to Complete My Griefwork	(to fill in later) The Results of My Griefwork

It may be helpful to talk to someone who is experienced
in assisting people in their work of grieving
to make your use of this chapter — and any other related parts
of this book — to be a more fully healing experience for you.
Such a person or people might include your therapist, counselor,
therapy group or the like.

Healthy grieving — to its completion — takes a lot of time.
So take a lot of time on working through this chapter.
Use your journal, diary or extra paper to write about
any experiences around your grieving.
This is in part why I and others suggest that in the best
full recovery program for being an adult child
or a co-dependent person it takes on average
from three to five years for us to heal ourself, our Child Within.
That grief work can include many if not all of the
principles and exercises described in this book.

As we grieve, we may discover that what works best
for us is the *opposite* of what we were taught about
how to handle a loss, hurt or trauma (see page 196).

We can now summarize some guidelines for **healthy** grieving.

Guidelines for Healthy Grieving

- **Accept my grief** — I need not deny or pretend.

- **Feel** — Let my feelings flow and feel them.

- **Don't try to replace** the loss immediately.

- **Let myself be with the pain** of the loss.

- **Talk with safe people** about my feelings around the loss.

- **Don't change the subject** if pain and grief come up.

- **Take good care of myself** — Nutrition, rest, moderate exercise.

- **Involve myself** in moderate work and meaningful activity.

- Have **fun** when it comes up. Laughter is okay.

- **Take as much time** as I need.

23

Working Through Core Issues

An **issue** is any conflict, concern or potential problem, whether conscious or unconscious, that is incomplete for us — or needs action or change. A **core** issue is one that comes up repeatedly for many of us. There are at least 15 core issues. These include:

- Control
- Trust
- Being real
- Feelings
- Low self-esteem
- Dependence

- Fear of abandonment
- All-or-none thinking and behaving
- High tolerance for inappropriate behavior
- Over-responsibility for others
- Neglecting my own needs
- Grieving my ungrieved losses
- Difficulty resolving conflict, giving love and receiving love.

These core issues tend to emerge especially from several areas of our recovery and life:

- **Relationships** — of any kind — with others, self and our Higher Power

- Doing **experiential recovery work** — throughout our healing

- **Feedback** given by our therapy group members, therapists, sponsors, friends and others, and

- **Insight** from reading, listening, reflecting upon or working through conflict.

Core issues can assist us in describing and framing some of the origins and dynamics of such concepts as our:

- Problems in living
- Day to day conflicts
- "Character defects" and
- Our struggle with our ego or false self.

There are several principles of core issues that are useful in our healing:

Principles of Core Issues in Recovery

1. Before we identify a core issue, most of its dynamics and effects are unconscious.

2. These dynamics and effects are often manifested by being a martyr or victim, and by enacting a repetition compulsion.

3. When working on material related to a core issue, it is useful eventually to *name* the specific core issue or issues.

4. It is useful to explore how the core issue came to be and how it manifested and still manifests in our life.

5. Bringing a core issue into our conscious awareness provides us the experience of the unfinished business, an improved psycho-spiritual understanding and a movement to self-actualization, integration, wholeness and sanity.

6. In working through the core issues, we connect the pain (of experiencing the dynamics in action that the core issue exposes) to how we were mistreated and how our True Self went into hiding.

7. Core issues usually have opposites or all-or-none type components (e.g., trust versus distrust).

8. Core issues can have at least four components: physical, mental, emotional and spiritual.

9. Focusing on a core issue sets in motion a flow to other issues, both core and non-core.

10. Core issues are also often inter-related with *basic dynamics* in relationships.

11. Most issues that we have with others, we also have with our self and with our Higher Power.

12. Our True Self uses recognizing and working through core issues for self-discovery, growth and returning Home (ego treats core issues as all-or-none, gets stuck in them as a martyr or victim).

While I describe these principles and each core issue
in more detail in *HCW* and in *Wisdom to Know the Difference,*
reviewing them may begin to raise our awareness of how
core issues affect us in our recovery.

It may be helpful now to review the names of the specific issues on
page 203.

Might any of these apply in any way to any aspect of your life?

To assist in answering, it may be helpful to review parts of Chapter
2 on What Is My Recovery Potential? The Recovery Potential
Survey (page 12) may help uncover some of these core issues and
also may help indicate how important each may be in our life.

Which of these core issues tend to affect me the most?

Use the space below to write each core recovery issue
in the order that it has most meaning for you in your life.
Place a number next to each, in order of its priority.

Core issues reflect some of our areas of conflict
as healthy human beings.
They show up for us in our day-to-day lives
in **countless ways**, including those areas
listed at the bottom of page 203 and the top of page 204.

When we are struggling with a particular problem or conflict,
knowing about using a core-issues approach to healing
will often facilitate our eventually applying a **name**
to one or more specific issues.
Once we thus name an issue, we can then begin to **focus**
on more of the **essentials** of our particular struggle.

Once focused, we are less and less distracted by nonessentials
and can thus **concentrate** on working to resolve the issue.

What we can **use** to do this work of resolving an issue includes any one or more of the many **experiential techniques** described in this book.

I describe some basic principles of using these *experiential techniques* throughout this book and especially in Chapters 17 and 18. On page 142 I list their four characteristics: **Being Real, Focused** on our **Inner Life, Structured** and doing our healing work through them in a **Safe** environment. We can use these four characteristics to assist us in working through each of our core issues.

As we name and work through a core issue, it can be most helpful to address it in a series of steps or stages.

Working Through a Problem, Conflict or Issue

1. **Identify** and name my **specific upset, problem** or **conflict.**
2. **Reflect** upon it from my powerful **inner life.**
3. **Talk about it** with **safe** people (i.e., tell that specific part of my story).
4. Ask for **feedback** from them.
5. **Name** the **core issue.**
6. **Talk** about it some **more.**
7. Ask for some more **feedback.**
8. Select an appropriate **experiential technique.**
9. Use that to **work** on your specific conflict and feelings at a deeper level.
10. **Talk** and/or **write** some **more** about it.
11. **Meditate** upon it or **pray** about it.
12. Consider how I might **learn** from it.
13. If I still feel incomplete, **repeat** any of the above.
14. Whenever I am ready, *Let it go.*

This approach can be used in concert with that presented in Chapter 17 on working through conflict and transference issues (pages 144 through 152).

Would your Child Within ever be interested in experimenting with such an approach whenever it might have a problem, upset, conflict or issue come up in its life? If its answer were "yes," then it might try to use this series of healing actions, starting from number one, and slowly and with patience, working through number 14. It might take days, weeks or even months or longer to work through a particular upset or conflict in this way.

Doing so offers the advantage of a high likelihood that you will complete much of your unfinished business around your upset or conflict, as well as the core issue or issues that may be intertwined with it.

Use the following chart to organize your work on these conflicts and issues.

Chart 23.1. Conflicts And Issues

Upset, Problem Or Conflict	Core Issue(s) Involved	Plan For Healing

As shown in Table 23.1 as we work through a specific core issue, we can do so in an *evolutionary sequence,* depending on *where* we might be in our healing around that particular core issue. *For example —*

1. *Early* in such evolution, we may be most interested in such healing actions as **questioning, risking, realizing, recognizing, identifying** and **defining.**

2. In the *Middle* stage of our healing around a core issue we may use **learning, practicing, clarifying, experiencing** and working at a **deeper** level.

3. During an *Advanced* stage we may begin to **consolidate** our **progressively increasing awareness** around the core issue, while using that awareness at **working through** upsets and conflicts without being a martyr or victim — **as a Hero/Heroine.**

4. When we are *recovered* we can **continue** using all of the above with still more **awareness, success** and **enjoyment.**

I describe these for each core issue on the next two pages, from page 109 of HCW.

Table 23.1. Some Steps in Transforming and Integrating Recovery Issues in Healing Our Child Within

Recovery Issues	Early	Middle	Advanced	Recovered
1. Grieving	Identifying our losses	Learning to grieve	Grieving	Grieving current losses
2. Being real	Identifying our real self	Risking being real	Practicing being real	Being real
3. Neglecting our own needs	Realizing we have needs	Identifying our needs	Beginning to get our needs met	Getting our needs met
4. Being over-responsible for others, etc.	Identifying boundaries	Clarifying boundaries	Learning to set limits	Being responsible for self, with clear boundaries
5. Low self-esteem	Identifying	Sharing	Affirming	Improved self-esteem
6. Control	Identifying	Beginning to let go	Taking responsibility	Taking responsibility while letting go
7. All-or-none	Recognizing and identifying	Learning *both/and* choices	Getting free	Freedom from all-or-none choices

8. Trust	Realizing trusting can be helpful	Trusting selectively	Learning to trust safe people	Trusting appropriately
9. Feeling	Recognizing and identifying	Experiencing	Using	Observing and using feelings
10. High tolerance for inappropriate behavior	Questioning what is appropriate and what is not	Learning what is appropriate and what is not	Learning to set limits	Knowing what is appropriate, or if not, asking a safe person
11. Fear of abandonment	Realizing we were abandoned or neglected	Talking about it	Grieving our abandonment	Freedom from fear of abandonment
12. Difficulty handling and resolving conflict	Recognizing and risking	Practicing expressing feelings	Resolving conflicts	Working through current conflicts
13/14. Difficulty giving and receiving love	Defining love	Practicing love	Forgiving and refining	Loving self, others, and Higher Power
15. Dependence	Identifying our dependence needs	Learning about healthy dependence and healthy independence	Practicing healthy dependence and independence	Being healthily dependent and independent

Use the space below to write about anything that comes up for you around any of these core issues.

I discuss core issues further in vols 1-3 of my taped workshops from ACCESS and in HCW and *Wisdom to Know the Difference* (see references).

24

Transforming And Integrating

When we transform, we make lemons into lemonade.

Working through our conflict, we become more aware,
responsible, empowered and free.

Transforming is a changing of form, a forming over, a restructuring.
Ultimately it is a shift of living our life to get somewhere
to living our life as our True Self — our Child Within.

When we transform, we transform our awareness or consciousness.
We switch from one domain of reality and being to another,
to a higher, more empowering, peaceful and creative level of being.
We consider more possibilities and have more choices.
We experience more personal power through having a greater
awareness of our inner life, combined with taking more
responsibility for using that inner life and making our lives work.

What we transform is the way we view, experience, handle
and live our life. Probably our greatest single transformation is when
we change our base of living from that of our false or co-dependent
self to that of our True Self.

We thus transform as follows —

| False or | to | True Self or |
| co-dependent self ————————————————————→ | | Child Within |

That is what this book, *HCW* and *WTKD* and adult child
and co-dependence recovery are all about.

We can also describe transforming as our moving *from* the martyr/
victim cycle *into* the Hero/Heroine's Journey,
about which Joseph Campbell and others have spoken and written.
The journey of recovery, of healing our Child Within,
is the Hero/Heroine's Journey of living authentically.
Transformation is the process and experience of moving
from the more limited martyr/victim cycle to becoming
more aware, responsible, empowered and free as a Hero/Heroine.
Some characteristics of each follow —

Martyr/Victim Cycle	Hero/Heroine's Journey
False self	True Self
Self-contraction	Self-expansion
There and then	Here and now
Unfinished business	Finished and finishing business
Few personal rights	Many personal rights
Stagnation, regression	Growth
Sharing little	Sharing as appropriate
Same story	Growing story
Repetition compulsion	Telling our story
Impulsive and compulsive	Spontaneous and flowing
Most is unconscious	Much is conscious
Unaware stuckness	Progressively aware becoming and being
Unfocused	Focused
Not working a recovery program	Working a recovery program
Less open to input from others	Open to input from safe others
Varying degrees of "dry drunk"	Working through pain and appreciating joy
Doing it "on my own"	Co-creatorship
Often grandiose	Humble yet confident
Fewer possibilities and choices	More possibilities and choices
"Unhappy dream"	"Happy dream" (A Course in Miracles)
Excludes Higher Power	Includes Higher Power
Illness	Health
Curse	Gift

Every exercise in this book helps us
in our process of transformation.

When you have some quiet time, look back through each of this
book's exercises and see if there are any that you have not yet
worked through. In the space below, write the page number and
a brief description of each exercise that you have not completed.

We can facilitate our healing by considering **why** we may not have
completed any parts of it. Some *possible blocks* to healing in a
particular area might include —

- **Fear** — of many things, such as the unknown, change, abandonment, rejection, mistreatment — or even of success.

- **Shame** — of who we think we are, thinking that we
  may not deserve to feel and get free.

- **Distrust** — or doubt about parts or even all of the process of
  our healing.

- **Confusion** — about many things, including what to do next.

- **Feeling overwhelmed** — about the healing or by any of these
  factors.

- **Lack of skills** — about what and how to do our healing.

- **No recovery plan** or an inactive one.

To help sort this out, assign a *number* to each of
the incomplete exercises that you listed above.

On the next page, write the number of each
and then some possible reasons why you might be
stuck or blocked about working them.

Chart 24.1. My Healing Block Checklist

Number	Possible Reasons Why Blocked	Plan to Get Free of Block

To help facilitate this process, **select someone safe** to tell about any stuckness or blocks that you might be or have been experiencing. Ask them for feedback, but not "free advice." (See page 116 for a description of constructive feedback.) When you have completed your telling and describing your blocks, and received some **feedback,** write a plan (in above chart) to help you get free so that you can complete any healing exercises that you may not have done.

How are you transforming? How have you grown?
Write whatever comes up for you in the space below.

Ask **safe others** for **feedback** as to how you've **changed** or **grown.** Write about that in the space below.

An advantage to working through a conflict is that
we free ourself from the bindings and shackles that it had on us.
We are then free to be more creative and experience our life
from a richer, more real and deeper dimension.
And we can forgive ourself for not being perfect.
All this healing work can be done inside and outside of
a full recovery program, as described throughout this book.

Integrating

Integrating means that we are now fully applying our healing and transformations to our daily life.

Integration means to make whole from separate parts.

When we reach and complete the integration stage of our recovery,
we can now handle an upset that used to take us
much longer to resolve — if at all — to resolve in a shorter time,
more efficiently and with far more awareness and responsibility.

By this stage we have progressively less and less confusion
and difficulty in using what we have worked through and learned.
Now we simply do what needs to be done,
almost as though by reflex.

While doing all of the above, we may still need
some assistance from our **support system.**

At the integration stage we are just who we are
and have no need to apologize to anyone for being ourself.
Now we can relax, play and have fun without fear, shame or guilt.
At the same time we have learned to set boundaries and limits
where doing so is appropriate for our needs.
We know and act upon our rights.

To help with transforming and integrating, I suggest that you review
the personal "Bill of Rights" on pages 115-117 of *HCW.*

The following is an exercise to refer to and use several times or more.

Over the next few months or longer, consider keeping a log of how you live your life and handle your upsets or conflicts.

Chart 24.2. When I Handle My Upsets or Conflicts

Upset Or Conflict	How Long I Used to Take	How Long I Take Now	What Has Made the Difference

25

Creating New Rules
And Messages

This chapter continues from the flow of this entire book
and especially from Chapter 8: "Did I Learn Any Rigid Rules
Or Negative Messages?" It may be helpful in getting the most
out of this chapter to review Chapter 8 briefly now (page 55).

Be sure that you have completed working through Chapter 8
before working through this one now.

Hidden in the almost overwhelming mass of recorded information
and teachings throughout the world is
a simple and powerful concept —

What we believe is what we get.

Our beliefs are stored mostly in our unconscious (sometimes called
subconscious) mind and to some extent in our conscious mind.
Our subconscious mind is automatic, like a computer,
because whatever it is fed or given is what it produces.

Through a series of energies, actions and events, our mind
compels us to create the conditions of our beliefs. For example,
if we believe that we are bad, inadequate, defective or not enough,
or that we will never be successful in and enjoy our life,
or any other belief _____,
                                    (fill in the blank)
then our subconscious mind is compelled to create the conditions
of that belief.

That is the **only thing** that it knows to do with a belief.

A belief thus becomes for us an *energy* that knows only
how to create itself as a reality in our life.

While the exact way that it creates this reality remains a mystery,
it appears to work through a series of energies and actions
that tend to unfold and flow according to the following pattern —

- Belief
  ↓
- Thoughts
  ↓
- Feelings
  ↓
- Decisions
  ↓
- Choices
  ↓
- Behavior
  ↓
- Life experience

The *energy* of any **belief** we have can give us only **thoughts** and
ideas that are in harmony with our belief. The *energy* of the
belief and the *energy* of these thoughts and ideas then compels
us to **feel** in a way that is also in harmony with them. And from
our feelings we tend to make our **decisions** and **choices**, which
then create our **behavior.** And from all of these, we then derive
our **life experience.**

The energy of any belief that we have surrounds us with the
people, places, things and conditions that are in harmony with
the belief. Our mind always finds a way to create the conditions
of our beliefs. That is how unlimited and creative we can be
when we . . .

Create a New Belief.

We were not born with our beliefs. Rather, our beliefs are a result of
other people's beliefs combined with the circumstances of our
past, whether painful or joyful.

But to survive, we had to adopt the beliefs of our family
and the beliefs of influential others. These beliefs
included in large part the rigid rules and negative messages
that we were **taught** and **learned,** and thus incorporated
into our view of ourself, others and our Higher Power.

If we learned and then adopted these beliefs,
that means that at some level we **chose** to believe them.
But in our past we didn't choose them voluntarily. Rather, we chose
them so that we could **survive** in a chaotic and painful world.

And if we learned, adopted and chose them, it means that,
even though it may have been *involuntary,* we *created* them.

And if we created them, we can dis-create them.

We can dis-create any belief that is not working for us or that is detrimental to the aliveness, growth and serenity of our Child Within.

To dis-create, we *stop creating* a belief.

Some techniques to dis-create a belief include to

1. **Experience** or re-experience whatever might have led us to
   come to that belief in the first place. (This book and *HCW*
   describe numerous ways to experience any unfinished business associated with any destructive or negative beliefs.) When
   we thus experience, we can complete it and then let go of it.

   Another way to dis-create a belief is to
2. **Ask for help** from our Higher Power through meditation or
   prayer. Selected guided imagery can also assist.
   And another way, realizing the ineffectiveness of the old belief,
   is to
3. **Create a new belief.**

A way to create one or more new beliefs is to consider
the following question (Palmer 1987) —

What would the person I would like to be believe?

It may be difficult to answer this question with complete satisfaction
if we have not worked a full recovery program in
healing our Child Within, as described in this book and *HCW.*
It may also be difficult if we have not worked through
Chapter 8 to a fair degree of completion.
If you have any doubts or questions about these difficulties, talk
to your therapy group, therapist or another safe person about them.

In the space at the top of the next page,
write your answers to this above question.
Before writing on the next page, however,
it may be helpful to explore and form your new (or old) beliefs
on a separate sheet of paper. When you have completed
these to your satisfaction, write them at the top of the next page.

What would the person I would like to be believe?

Healing Self-Talk

Like affirmations, I first communicate my beliefs
from my **self** to my **self.** When I talk to myself
in this way, I am saying, "This is the way it is for me."
Which translates, "This is my **reality** right now."
And that reality which I have thus created will exist for me
in some fashion or other for as long as I hold that belief.

As I heal my Child Within, I can communicate my new and healing
beliefs to myself in some of the following ways —
  • Imagine them
  • Write them in this book and in other handy places
  • Display them prominently in places that I can see easily
    (making sure that no unsafe or toxic people see them,
    so that they won't try to talk me out of them in any way).
  • Record my voice saying them in a convincing manner,
    over and over, and play that back to myself frequently.
    I can play them just before I go to sleep, just when I awaken
    and just before I meditate or pray.
  • As I meditate, visualize myself enacting these healing beliefs.

As I create and use my new beliefs, I take as much time as I need.
There is absolutely no rush to accomplish any of these.

As I repeat a belief in these ways, it becomes progressively
and comfortably implanted in my subconscious mind.
And once it is there, my subconscious mind automatically acts,
over time, to make it a healing reality for me.

Healing Talk with Safe Others

Having put some of the above into practice, I am now ready to
   begin to reinforce and strengthen this belief by communicating it
   to safe others.

I can ask any safe person(s) in my life, such as my therapy group,
   my therapist, sponsor, best friend or Higher Power to listen while
   I **say** my new and healing beliefs to them. As I say *with conviction*
   each belief, I attentively **observe my inner life.**

Taking each belief, one at a time, as I say each out loud,
I can ask myself the following questions about each —

What is coming up in my inner life each time that I say each belief?

Do I feel convinced about that belief?

If not, what might possibly be interfering with my conviction?

Some possible interfering factors include:
any old, rigid rule or negative belief, any doubt, fear, worry or
other thought, sensation or other distraction.

I can then begin to *watch* and *experience* that interfering distraction.
When I get a sense of that interfering distraction,
I can then describe it to the person who is listening.
And to help get free of the distraction, as I describe it to them,
it is useful to *exaggerate* the interfering distraction,
both within my inner life and outwardly to them,
with words, sentences, sounds, actions, gestures or dramatizations.
I could even write out some of these distractions and in a special
ceremony, rip them up and throw them away or burn them.

I *exaggerate* in this way so that I can more fully experience
the distraction, over and over, until my experience of it
begins to become more and more complete (Palmer 1987).
I can then ask the listening safe person or persons for some
feedback in the form of what they see or hear,
without any judgment, criticism or advice.

I can do such an exercise any number of times.

As I do so, I will become progressively more convinced that
that new belief is true for me now.

And once my belief becomes true for me from inside,
it gradually becomes my reality.

When I (CLW) personally completed the above exercises,
some of the beliefs that I created were —

I am part of my Higher Power.
I am a Child of my Higher Power.
I get my needs met.
I experience and handle my painful feelings
   in a healthy way, as they come up.
I let be and enjoy my healthy joyful feelings.
I love my Child Within.
I love others.
I love my Higher Power.
I create no unnecessary suffering for myself.
I experience, complete and heal my past woundedness as it comes
   up.
I am experiencing and completing what I came to earth to do.

These are beliefs that came up for me, and I in no way
suggest or expect anyone to try to have my beliefs.
I include them here as *examples only,* so that you
can more easily create your own original and special beliefs.

A word of caution:

There are several commercially available structured experiences that address our beliefs in a sincere effort in helping us with introspection and realizing more of our human potential. Some of these include: The Forum (formerly est), Insight, Lifespring, New Identity, Scientology, Avatar and others. Some advantages of these include that they are relatively brief, in part experiential, and founded upon mostly sound psychological and metaphysical principles. Some disadvantages are that they are often run by non-clinicians, may be expensive and in varying degrees may have a relatively weak screening procedure for and attention to people's special and individual needs. Perhaps their strongest disadvantages can be that some of these may be narrow in their focus, neglecting some important areas of healing our Child Within, and at times tend to promote all-or-none thinking and behaving. This latter disadvantage can at times result in an unhealthy dependence upon beliefs and techniques taught and upon the organization, trainer or guru. While it may have started out to help the person, in its extreme it can end up distracting the person from healing their Child Within and thus realizing their True Self.

Based on my personal experience of participating in several of these commercially available, structured experiences as well as assisting several of my patients who spontaneously and voluntarily did one or more of them also, it is my clinical opinion that these can at times be risky and even dangerous unless they are done while in the context of a full recovery program for healing our Child Within. And even if the person is in such a full recovery program, a relapse into an unhealthy dependence upon the commercial experience may result to the degree that they drop out of their full recovery program. By saying the above, I am neither recommending for nor against any of them. My purpose, rather, is to alert anyone whose goal is to heal their Child Within about these potential disadvantages that can interfere with their healing, should they ever choose to try any of them.

Notes

26

Lightening Up
And Having Fun

To play and have fun is a healthy human need.

But to survive, we had to be serious.

We may have felt a need to be responsible and "in control."
We may have felt too conflicted to let go and have fun.
And we might have learned that if we were to lighten up
and have some fun — or to feel even comfortable —
that something bad might happen.

So most of the time we held our playful Child inside of us.

Or going to the opposite extreme, we may have
used humor and joking as a kind of defense against our pain.
But the pain would never really go away.

Learning to lighten up and have fun can be helped by considering some of the following. (Write any of your responses in the spaces.)

1. Do you remember as a child when your make-believe play took more time than any other kind of play?

   About how old were you? What made this change?

2. When did you play with stuffed toys or dolls?

   When did you stop?

3. Did any adults play imaginatively with you?

   Who were they?

4. Who older than you modeled playfulness?

   Was it healthy?

5. At what age were you taught about winning or losing games?

   What were the games?

6. When did you sing, color or draw expressively with no concern about whether you were doing it correctly?

7. What happened when you made a mistake while playing in your family?

   In your neighborhood?   At school?

8. What special talents, skills, handicaps or other qualities helped or hindered you in your social play?

9. Did you have enough playtime?   Enough playmates?

10. What did you learn about playing and having fun from your family?

11. Did you have any traumatic or hurtful experiences, such as being bullied, isolated from a clique, teased or dominated?

What were they?

Who was there to protect you?

What residual effects have these events left?

12. What kind of jokes did you like?

   What was the role of humor in your childhood?

   How often did you laugh?

13. What did you learn about recreation and relaxation from your family and from your childhood?

   What have you learned as an adult?

14. Did you exercise or play any sports as a child or adolescent? What were they?

   Which ones were just for fun and non-competitive?

15. What did you learn about vacations as a child?

   What were your vacations like?

   How has that affected your vacations as an adult?

16. What experiences in your school, church or clubs helped or inhibited your spontaneity?

17. On balance, what did you learn about play and humor?

   What have you learned as an adult?

These questions are modified from Blatner and Blatner, 1988.

What was it like for you to read these questions?

What was it like to answer them?

As with other experiential exercises, it can be helpful
and healing to find a safe person and tell them
about your answers to some of these questions.
Who do you have in mind who you could talk to?

Several factors may *stifle* or *block* our *ability to lighten up*
and have fun. Each of these may be a manifestation
of a wounded Child who is in hiding —

- Predominance of our false, adapted or co-dependent self
- Needing to be "in control"
- Never having been shown or taught how to have fun
- Difficulty trusting
- Tendency to look outside of ourself for happiness and fulfillment
- Shyness or shame when with others
- Restriction of play to structured or competitive activities

Make a check mark next to any of those factors
that you can identify with.

We may have had no one model the joy of being a grownup,
including how to lighten up and play in a healthy way
— like Mary Poppins, Auntie Mame or Zorba the Greek.

Healthy humor and play are healing.
They tend to bring out the Child inside us.
Play is a necessity to heal and to stay healthy.

Some characteristics of play include that it is —

- **Spontaneous** — while it can be planned and structured, much of play and recreation are spontaneous. Whatever comes up that is light, playful and creative in our Child can come out. Spontaneity is different from unhealthy impulsiveness, which may be demanding, attacking, controlling or manipulating. Spontaneity is inviting but non-demanding, non-controlling and not manipulative.

- **Individual** — To lighten up and have fun is not characterized by what others do or think we should do. We enjoy ourself in our own unique way, doing exactly what may spontaneously come up for us.

- **Transcends the ordinary** — including our ordinary state of mind and our ordinary activities.

- **Light** — the mood is light and not at all serious.

- **Creative** — Our Child Within creates whatever it will as it plays in whatever way it may play.

- **Fun** — Play is enjoyable. We get pleasure from doing it. Needing no justification, it is just plain fun.

- **Not harmful** — like two puppies or kittens at play, play is not harmful to ourself or to others.

Humor and Laughter

Have you had a good belly laugh lately?

Have you ever laughed so hard that your sides ached?

Humor and laughter can strengthen our immune system and help us heal all sorts of illness. But like most things in life, at times these can also be unhealthy, depending on how we use them.

For example, *laughing at* someone may be destructive in the long run, whereas *laughing with* someone can be healing.

I show some characteristics of these two kinds of humor below.

Table 26.1. Healing Humor Guidelines*

Laughing With Others	Laughing At People, Feelings or Issues
1. Going for the jocular vein	1. Going for the jugular vein
2. Caring	2. Contempt
3. Put up	3. Put down
4. Empathy	4. Lack of sensitivity
5. Brings people closer	5. Divides people
6. Involves people in the fun	6. Excludes people
7. Making the choice to be the "butt"	7. Having no choice in being the "butt"
8. Builds confidence	8. Destroys self-esteem
9. Invites people	9. Offends people
10. Leads to positive repartee	10. Leads to one-downsmanship cycle
11. Can involve laughing at yourself	11. Always involves laughing at others
12. Supportive	12. Sarcastic
13. Facilitative or focusing	13. Distracting

Some of us may have grown up around a lot of the unhealthy kind of humor, where people laughed at one another. And so it may be difficult for us to joke and laugh about anything.

Did anything like that ever happen to you?
(Use the space below to write about your experiences.)

*From *Laughing Matters*, courtesy of Joel Goodman (no. 13 my addition).

It may be healing to review this chapter now
and from time to time, discuss any aspects of it
that you like with a safe person.
This may include your counselor, therapist,
therapy group, self-help group or best friend.
Take as much time as you need.

Based on what you have learned and experienced
so far about the healing aspects of lightening up
and having fun, are there any changes you'd
like to make in your day-to-day life?

Use the space below to write anything you'd like.

Notes

27

Spirituality

Spirituality is a powerful force in healing our Child Within.
Yet many of us have a hard time making it work for us.

To what might that be due?

I have identified at least 12 blocks over which we adult children
can stumble on our healing journey to realizing spirituality and
serenity.

Blocks to Realizing Spirituality and Serenity

1. **We don't know what spirituality is.**
   We can start by saying that it is about our relationships with our
   self, others and our Higher Power.
   It expands in proportion to our awareness
   and our personal and experiential relationships with these three.
   If convenient, I suggest reading Chapter 15
   "The Role of Spirituality" in *HCW.* If interested in more,
   read *Spirituality in Recovery* and *Emmanuel's Book II.*

2. **We confuse spirituality with organized religion.**
   While it includes, nurtures and supports organized religion,
   as it does most everything in the universe,
   it *transcends* organized religion.
   Spirituality is far deeper and richer.

3. **Associate Higher Power with "parents,"** like our
   "father," "mother" or other authority figures.
   Could it be that we project or transfer onto our Higher Power
   much of our unfinished business?
   If we do, we may project —

4. **Resentment** at our Higher Power.
Some reasons may include that we may believe
that God has punished us for
being bad, or that we are angry or resentful at It (God)
for sending us into such a troubled family and life.
Related to all this is that we may —

5. **Have negative, preconceived notions** of Higher Power
— e.g., an angry or unavailable One. We may have
been taught this by authority figures, including some
biblical writers and clergy who themselves may have been
or are unhealed adult children, projecting these notions
onto *their* Higher Power.

6. **I may be unaware of who I really am** —
i.e., my True Self, my Child Within. Identifying with my false or co-
dependent self, I may not be aware of my integrity, wholeness
and sanity — as the Second Step addresses.
This unawareness may be related to the fact that we —

7. **Have not healed our Child Within,** i.e., have not
done our basic adult child recovery work.
This may include not having done basic stage one
recovery work, including working the Twelve Steps.
Or we may be —

8. **Stuck in the martyr/victim stance** or cycle (see pages 190
and 212, plus *WTKD*).
We may be able to feel only mostly painful
feelings or numbness, and not be aware
of our inner life and how we can enter and flow through
our Hero/Heroine's Journey.
No matter which stage we may be in,
our Hero/Heroine's Journey
is the journey of recovery. All of
the material, techniques and skills that I describe
in my writings, and that you can read in others,
describes this process.

Another block may be that we —

9. **Won't take responsibility for our life.**
   Related to many of the above blocks, we may use
   this block because we are just accustomed or even addicted to
   believing and acting as though we can't make our life work.
   We may not know that we can stop
   blaming others and the universe, and that
   we can take responsibility for making an enjoyable success
   out of our life.
   We may also be using —

10. **No, or ineffective, spiritual practices.**
    This one and many of the above blocks
    may be associated with our having had —

11. **No joyful spiritual experiences.**

    We may also be —

12. **Unaware of our Co-creatorship** with our Higher Power.
    Co-creatorship means that in concert with
    our Higher Power, we take responsibility for creating our life.

Many colleagues and I believe that all of these blocks
are aggravated by the conventional Judeo-Christian-Islamic ethic
with all its trappings of guilt, shame, and fear
and by conventional psychology and
our conventional health and mental health delivery systems.

But there is a way out and that is to heal our Child Within,
and to continue to work a long-term recovery program that includes
an increasing spiritual awareness.

Write in the space below anything you like that may be coming up.

Did you identify with any of the above blocks?
If so, would you be interested in making a plan to get free of
each one?
Feel free to use the space below to write your plan.

Chart 27.1. Getting Free Of Blocks to Spirituality

Block	Plan to Get Free

I believe that once we heal our Child Within
and connect it to our Higher Power,
we will experience our spirituality and
serenity automatically and naturally.

We can now begin to summarize our journey,
which may occur sequentially along the following
twelve levels or stages.

The Child Within's Psycho-Spiritual Journey

Corresponding Recovery Stage

Adult child wounding
↓
Emptiness (loss of our True Self)
↓
Attempts to fill the emptiness   0
    (through co-dependence, addictions and compulsions)
↓
Frustration at looking for fulfillment
    outside of us   1
↓
Heal our Child Within, which includes
and results in —   2
↓
   Healthy boundaries
↓
Self Knowledge and authentic life experience
↓
Personal experience of Higher Power   3
↓
Connect Child with Higher Power
↓
   Co-creatorship
↓   ↘
Accept what   Change what can
cannot change
    ↘   ↙
Peace and Serenity

Daily spiritual practice tends to *facilitate* us on this journey.

This journey is usually more circular than the linear
way described above.
This is because we can "cycle through it"
at any time in the course of our daily, weekly and monthly life.
By recognizing where we *are* according to these levels,
we can focus on that level,
consciously work through any conflict around that level,
and then move to the next. Using the
principles described in this book and elsewhere
can facilitate that work.

In recovery there is often a temptation to try to move quickly
from the early levels or stages to the more advanced.
We would like to jump
from the pain and confusion of our emptiness and our
frustration directly into the peace and serenity,
and bypass the middle stages. But when we do that,
we abandon our Child Within and thereby all its
power, creativity and rich experience.

We can call that jumping or bypassing "premature transcendence"
or "high level denial."
It can occur in many situations, such as in cults,
born-again experiences, guru addiction, and in using
all sorts of methods (e.g., see cautions on pages 133, 165, 223),
and jumping too fast into advanced spiritual techniques and paths.

In short, even otherwise authentic spiritual experiences
can at times distract us from living as our True Self.

Being a successful human being requires
a delicate balance and an integration of all
of our levels of consciousness, awareness or being.

That is Sanity.

I wish you the very best on your journey.

It is all spiritual.

28

Loving My Child Within

Can it be useful in my healing to learn to love myself?

My sense is that Unconditional Love is
the most powerful healing and creative energy in the universe.
And that Love energy exists naturally inside each of us.
In this final healing of our Child Within
we can open ourselves to this Love.

We adult children have often been taught
that to love ourself is somehow bad, even a sin.

Yet this notion is the *opposite* of what we now know
about what is most healing for our Child Within.

How could such a notion have come into existence?

In the sections that follow I borrow from Gay Hendricks,
who summarized this crucial concept in his book.

Crosby observes that the reason we do not love ourselves is not so much that we do not know how but that we have a belief that it is wrong to have self-esteem. He traces this belief through Western culture back to certain parts of the Bible in which an idol was defined as anything that could claim the allegiance and loyalty of the human heart. To prevent people from elevating the self to a position rivaling that of God, the early church fathers began to characterize the self as unclean, sinful, in need of redemption. The self was off to a bad start in every possible way.

What is the basis for this attitude? Dr. Crosby points out that there are two accounts of creation in Genesis. The one in the first chapter is dramatically different from that in the second chapter.

The Views in Chapter One	The Views in Chapter Two
God is humanistic.	God is authoritarian.
Creation is a good thing.	Creation is a test for Adam and Eve.
God is egalitarian.	God is patriarchal and uses woman as an agent for Adam's sin.
God makes man and woman in his own image.	No image mentioned, only punishment for transgression.

We can only guess at the reasons the early church fathers made the second creation story the cornerstone of Christian dogma. First, they probably did not feel very good about themselves. It would be difficult for someone who felt good to embrace such a bleak view of the human condition. Second, if one were interested in building up a strong church, one would find it an advantage to have constituents who felt in strong need of redemption. If people can be led to believe that they are sunk deep in sin and that the church is the means of redemption, a prosperous future for the church is virtually assured. Recall also that these were rough, often savage times, when a benign version of the human condition would be hard to support. For these and other reasons Western culture was built upon the foundation of a remarkably negative view of the self. Subsequent religious movements, such as the Protestant Reformation of Luther, Puritanism and the Methodist movement of Wesley, sought to get back to an even bleaker view of ourselves. Catholic or Protestant, the view was the same: man is a depraved sinner in need of redemption. (And what of other religions? — CIW)

With such a negative view in circulation for the past two thousand years, we must give ourselves credit for even entertaining the idea of loving ourselves.

All these things we have learned. We see the world exactly upside down. Our task is to set our vision straight again. Let's see if we can identify some basic attitudes that will set us free.

> I have learned to see the world the way it isn't.
> I have done this for my survival.
> I am now interested in much more than survival.
> I can see it the way it is.
> There is nothing outside myself that can save me.
> I have everything I need inside me.
> All the love I have been searching for is here within me.
> I demand it from others because I am unwilling to give it to myself.
> I can give it to myself.
> My very nature is love, so there is no need to search for it, no need to work at it.
> Love is the only thing I need to change.
> I am now willing to love myself.

With these new beliefs, we can now consider the following exercise.

1. Notice your present state of mind or feeling. It could be mad, scared, joyous, hating yourself, bored, neutral.
2. Love yourself for what you are experiencing. It matters not if you do not know how to love yourself. At first just say the words if you can't figure out how. Say, "I love myself for (not being able to love myself, being scared, feeling happy, etc.)." After a while you will probably identify a physical sensation of loving yourself.
3. Stay with it as long as it feels interesting and comfortable.
4. Remember, you don't need to go around loving yourself all the time for your life to work wonderfully. You just have to go around being willing to love yourself. Willingness lets you flow with the stream rather than against it.

What was it like to do this exercise?
If you are experiencing any blocks or difficulties or anything from your inner life, describe it in the space below.

Look at the following table, reading from the bottom up.

Table 28.1. The Transition from Nonexperience to Experience

Experience	8. Being willing to be the source of love for yourself and others. 7. Being willing to personally *experience* loving yourself. 6. *Accepting* things the way they are (e.g., you don't love yourself, you have a lot of reasons why you don't love yourself, you are afraid of loving yourself).
Non-experience	5. *Reasoning* that you are lovable. 4. *Believing* that you should love yourself. 3. *Deciding* you will love yourself. 2. *Wishing* you could love yourself. 1. *Hoping* you can love yourself.

Below the line is the realm of nonexperience. The first act of getting above the line is to see things the way they are. In other words, to get out of the mud, one must first acknowledge that one *is* stuck in the mud. Hoping you are not stuck will not help, nor will wishing, believing, deciding or being reasonable about it. To acknowledge that one is stuck in the mud has power because it leads to other key questions. How stuck am I? How can I get out? Do I need help or can I do it myself? What can this experience teach me about living? It is an odd paradox that only by inquiry into the mud can we get to the light.

So much energy goes into pretending to ourselves and others that we are not stuck in the mud that we spin our wheels furiously, to the mud spattered chagrin of the bystanders in our life.

Once we get above the line, life goes a little smoother. We feel more, we see more, we hear more. Of course, not all of it is pleasant, but at least it is real. After the years and decades we have spent in the illusory world of our hopes and beliefs, reality has a refreshing clarity and power to it, even if some of it is unpleasant.

"The surest test if a man be sane," says the Chinese Book of Tao, "is if he accepts life whole, as it is."

Accepting life whole, as it is, not only restores our sanity but also puts us in the line for the higher experiences of life, such as the one listed at the top of the preceding table. A height in experience is to be willing to be the source of love for yourself and others. To be the source of love means that you are no longer striving for love: you are love. When you are fully open to love, you can provide an endless supply of it for yourself and others.

It may be useful eventually to read the short section on Love in *HCW* (pages 132-4) and the longer one in *Spirituality in Recovery*.

Tuning into this love energy is an *experiential* process. I open myself to *feeling* it. And to experiencing it in my heart and soul, in the deepest fiber of my being.

Since who I am is my Child Within, with all its abilities, power, dimensions and creativity, when I love myself, I love my Child Within.

Hendricks (1981), Hay (1988) and the Serenity Prayer suggest the following steps in loving myself.

Some Steps In Loving Myself

1. Stop all self-criticism.

2. Stop scaring myself with fear thoughts.

3. Be gentle, kind and patient with myself.

4. Stop needing to be perfect.

5. Support myself.

6. Ask for help with a safe support system.

7. Love my "negatives" (mistakes, shadow, painful feelings, etc.).

8. Care for my body (right nutrition, exercise, etc.).

9. Mirror work.

10. Accept the things I cannot change.

11. Change the things I can.

12. Begin loving myself right now, unconditionally.

Write your reaction to any of these in the space below.

The mirror work statements are from Hay (1988).

Although difficult to do, I can stand in front of a mirror,
looking at myself with all compassion,
and say any of the following.

Hay suggests that we do this healing exercise daily.

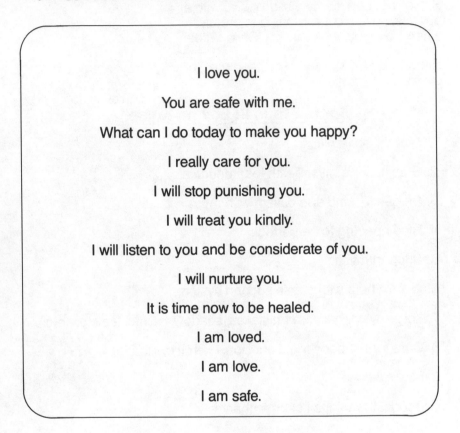

I love you.

You are safe with me.

What can I do today to make you happy?

I really care for you.

I will stop punishing you.

I will treat you kindly.

I will listen to you and be considerate of you.

I will nurture you.

It is time now to be healed.

I am loved.

I am love.

I am safe.

Figure 28.1. Mirror Work Statements

Which of the possibilities in this chapter are you willing to consider?

Which are you willing to do for your Child Within?

Are you worthy of this love?

29

Knowing When I Have
Healed My Child Within

Throughout this book I have suggested that on average
working through the most complete full recovery program
takes about three to five years to heal our Child Within.
Of course, this is just a range. I have seen one person
out of about 200 really complete their work in two years,
and many who completed theirs in longer than five years.
And I have seen many who have discontinued
their healing process — for varying lengths of time —
before they had completed their healing work.

How can I know if I have completed my healing?
While there are no sure criteria for making such a determination,
knowing what we do today about recovery
from a number of conditions,
including the adult child syndrome and co-dependence,
we can begin to consider some factors that may assist us.

I list these on the next page.

Some Factors in Determining When
I Have Healed My Child Within

1. Completed recovery goals about 90%.

2. Getting needs met regularly.

3. Seeing progressively more possibilities and choices.

4. Making healthy choices.

5. Able to set boundaries and limits when appropriate.

6. Transformed martyr/victim stance to Hero/Heroine's Journey.

7. Addictions and repetition compulsions close to zero.

8. Grieving losses healthily as appropriate.

9. A minimum of unnecessary pain and suffering.

10. Forgiveness and compassion for self and others.

11. Openness to learning (humility) and growth.

12. Able to laugh, play and have fun.

13. Experientially realize spirituality and serenity.

14. Able to love and be loved.

To achieve these may be quite an accomplishment
for anyone to do even in one lifetime, much less in three to five years.

- So use these as **guidelines** for considering whether
  you are ready to discontinue the intensity
  of your full recovery program,
  including weekly group and/or individual therapy.

- Review whether you have completed your **recovery goals**
  (page 121).

- Review whether you have **worked through most** of this book
  (page 211-213).

- Talk all of this over with your **therapy group** and/or individual
  therapist.

- Discuss it with other safe people who are in recovery.

As you consider all of the above, use the next page
to write about anything that may come up for you.

Notes

Gentle Reminders

Even after we have healed our Child Within and are feeling good
about ourself and our life, we may "relapse"
or fall back into some of those
old self-destructive habits or patterns. While these can be painful,
they can also be "gentle reminders"
that we are getting off the healthy track
of being real with ourself and safe others. And off the healthy track of
taking responsibility for working through our conflicts and
co-creating our life with our Higher Power.

Below are some of these gentle reminders.

As you study these, consider which ones
you may have experienced
in the past (make an "X" mark next to these)
and which ones you might be most prone to experience
in the future (make a check mark next to these).

Gentle Reminders — Some Relapse Warning Signs in Co-dependence

Loss of awareness of presence of True Self (Child Within)

Neglecting needs

Neglecting self-caring (rest, nutrition, exercise, intimacy)

Overdoing it

Medicating feelings

Active addictions, compulsions or attachments arise or return

Self-esteem lowers, or grandiosity

Choicemaking narrows

Loss of spontaneity and playfulness

Isolation

Loss of healthy boundaries or ability to set limits

Unhandled feelings

Unhandled stress (distress)

Defensiveness

Blaming others

Building resentments

Need to control people, places and things

Loss of connection with Higher Power

Stop using support systems

All-or-none thinking or behaving

People-pleasing

Irritability to an inappropriate extent

Frequent or persistent confusion or inability to make decisions

Frequent or persistent return of original or new symptoms (physical, mental, emotional or spiritual)

As any of these may come up in your life, use the chart
on the next page to write their name and a plan that would be
beneficial for your ongoing self-caring and healing.

Chart 29.1. Relapse Care

"Gentle Reminder" — Relapse Warning Sign	Plan for Self-Caring and Healing

When any of these comes up for us
we have now learned that we do not have to
beat ourself up over it. As long as we are human,
these kinds of things will be happening.
To help avoid unnecessary pain and suffering,
we can recognize them when they come up
and use them in our life, in our relationships with our self,
others and our Higher Power.

At the same time, there may be a loss, hurt
or trauma that we do need to grieve.
Or we may have a conflict that we need to work through.
Or someone might be mistreating us.
Or we might have lapsed in our crucial self-caring.

Use any of the healing methods in this book, in *HCW*
or from any other sources that may work for you.

> *In concert with my Higher Power,*
> *I am now the co-creator of my life.*

I wish you and your Child Within — which you now know
are the same Being — all the best in your adventure of Life.

Charlie Whitfield

Appendix 1

My Family Tree

Starting with yourself, inside the circle write the name, the age and in it or next to it write any outstanding or memorable characteristics of that person. Use any of the following abbreviations:

Alcsm = Alcoholism
CD = other Chemical Dependence
AC = Adult Child
CG = Compulsive Gambler
Wksm = Workaholism
Viol = Violence or physical abuse

SA = Sexual Addiction
Co-dep = Co-dependent
RA = Religious Addiction
SR = Strict Religious
ED = Eating Disorder
DF = Dysfunctional Family

Rgsm = Rage-aholism
In = Incest
Ca = Cancer
MI = Mental Illness
Su = Suicide
VA = Verbal Abuse

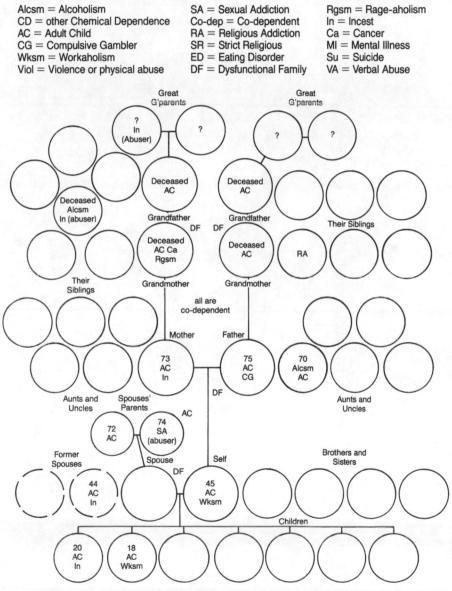

Appendix 2

Family Drinking Survey

	YES	NO
1. Does someone in your family undergo personality changes when he or she drinks to excess?	___	___
2. Do you feel that drinking is more important to this person than you are?	___	___
3. Do you feel sorry for yourself and frequently indulge in self-pity because of what you feel alcohol is doing to your family?	___	___
4. Has some family member's excessive drinking ruined special occasions?	___	___
5. Do you find yourself covering up for the consequences of someone else's drinking?	___	___
6. Have you ever felt guilty, apologetic or responsible for the drinking of a member of your family?	___	___
7. Does one of your family member's use of alcohol cause fights and arguments?	___	___
8. Have you ever tried to fight the drinker by joining in the drinking?	___	___
9. Do the drinking habits of some family members make you feel depressed or angry?	___	___
10. Is your family having financial difficulties because of drinking?	___	___
11. Did you ever feel like you had an unhappy home life because of the drinking of some members of your family?	___	___
12. Have you ever tried to control the drinker's behavior by hiding the car keys, pouring liquor down the drain, etc.?	___	___
13. Do you find yourself distracted from your responsibilities because of this person's drinking?	___	___
14. Do you often worry about a family member's drinking?	___	___
15. Are holidays more of a nightmare than a celebration because of a family member's drinking behavior?	___	___
16. Are most of your drinking family member's friends heavy drinkers?	___	___
17. Do you find it necessary to lie to employers, relatives or friends in order to hide your spouse's drinking?	___	___
18. Do you find yourself responding differently to members of your family when they are using alcohol?	___	___
19. Have you ever been embarrassed or felt the need to apologize for the drinker's actions?	___	___
20. Does some family member's use of alcohol make you fear for your own safety or the safety of other members of your family?	___	___

	YES	NO

21. Have you ever thought that one of your family members had a drinking problem? ___ ___

22. Have you ever lost sleep because of a family member's drinking? ___ ___

23. Have you ever encouraged one of your family members to stop or cut down on his or her drinking? ___ ___

24. Have you ever threatened to leave home or to leave a family member because of his or her drinking? ___ ___

25. Did a family member ever make promises that he or she did not keep because of drinking? ___ ___

26. Did you ever wish that you could talk to someone who could understand and help the alcohol-related problems of a family member? ___ ___

27. Have you ever felt sick, cried or had a "knot" in your stomach after worrying about a family member's drinking? ___ ___

28. Has a family member ever failed to remember what occurred during a drinking period? ___ ___

29. Does your family member avoid social situations where alcoholic beverages will not be served? ___ ___

30. Does your family member have periods of remorse after drinking occasions and apologize for his or her behavior? ___ ___

31. Please write any symptoms or medical or nervous problems that you have experienced since you have known your heavy drinker? (Write on back if more space needed.) ___ ___

If you answer "YES" to any 2 of the above questions, there is a good possibility that someone in your family may have a drinking problem.

If you answer "YES" to 4 or more of the above questions, there is a definite indication that someone in your family *does* have a drinking problem.

(These survey questions are modified or adapted from the Children of Alcoholics Screening Test (CAST), the Howard Family Questionnaire, and the Family Alcohol Quiz from Al-Anon.)

References

Abrams J, (ed): **Reclaiming The Inner Child.** Tarcher, Los Angeles, 1990. A concentrated collection of writings on the Child Within by 20th century authors.

Adult Children of Alcoholics (ACA — Central Service Board), Box 35623, Los Angeles, CA.

Al-Anon Family Groups, P.O. Box 182, Madison Square Station, New York, NY 10159.

Anonymous: **The Urantia (Earth) Book.** Urantia Foundation, 533 Diversey Pkwy, Chicago, IL 60614, 1955. A holy book that many believe is a spiritual milestone.

Bettelheim B: "The Importance of Play." *Atlantic Monthly,* Mar 1987. Some principles of play as a child that may be useful for our Child Within to know and experience.

Blatner A, Blatner, A: **The Art Of Play:** An Adult's Guide to Reclaiming Imagination and Spontaneity. Human Sciences Press, New York, 1988.

Bowden JD and Gravitz HL: **Genesis.** Health Communications, Pompano Beach, FL, 1987.

Bruckner-Gordon F, Gangi BK, Wallman GU: **Making Therapy Work:** Your Guide to Choosing, Using and Ending Therapy. Harper & Row, San Francisco, 1988. Most useful for individual therapy or counseling, somewhat useful for group therapy.

Campbell J. With Bill Moyers: **The Power Of Myth.** Doubleday, New York, 1988. A description in question and answer form of the Hero/Heroine's Journey from a world mythological perspective, from an author who was probably our greatest student and teacher of story and myth. Also available on videotape from PBS.

Capacchione L: **The Power Of Your Other Hand:** A Course in Channeling the Inner Wisdom of the Right Brain. Newcastle, N. Hollywood, CA, 1988.

Cermak TL: **Diagnosing and Treating Co-dependence.** Johnson Institue, Minneapolis, MN, 1986.

Co-Dependents Anonymous (CoDA), Box 33577, Phoenix, AZ 85067-3577, 602-944-0141.

Cohen H: **The Incredible Credible Cosmic Consciousness Diet.** Psychodynamics Press, Beverly Hills, CA, no date given. Clear description in calligraphy/verse of how beliefs create reality.

Colgrove M, Bloomfield H, McWilliams J: **How To Survive The Loss Of A Love.** Bantam Books, New York, 1976. Reading this book helps facilitate nearly any grieving process.

A Course In Miracles. Foundation for Inner Peace, Tiburon, CA, 1976. A modern holy book on spiritual psychology, forgiveness and inner peace. I recommend working its curriculum after completing a full recovery program, as described in this book. Also available on audiotape, which I recommend if you can afford its $140 price (well worth it if learn well by listening).

Crosby J: "On the origin of the taboo against self-love." *The Humanist,* Nov/Dec 1979, p. 45-47. A concise description of this major cultural and religious block to our healing and serenity.

Curran: **Traits Of A Healthy Family.** Harper & Row, 1983.

Defoore B: **Nurturing Your Inner Child** (audiotape). Institute for Personal and Professional Development, 4201 Wingren, Ste. 201-W, Irving, TX 75062, 800-322-4773, 1988.

Deikman AJ: **The Observing Self.** Beacon Press, Boston, MA, 1982. A clear and documented description of this powerful part of us, written by a transpersonal psychiatrist.

Diamond J: **Looking For Love In All The Wrong Places:** Overcoming Romantic and Sexual Addictions. Putnam's, New York, 1988. A concise and readable description and how to get free.

Figley CR, Scrignar CB, Smith WH: "PTSD: The Aftershocks of Trauma." *Patient Care,* May 15, 1988. A brief review from a medical and psychological perspective; includes a symptom inventory checklist that may supplement some of the exercises in Chapter 11 of this book.

Finn CC: Poem previously unpublished by author and published several times, attributed to "Anonymous" by others. Written in Chicago, 1966. Here published by permission of the author, personal communication, Fincastle, VA, Mar 1986 and Feb 1989.

Friends in Recovery: **The Twelve Steps — A Way Out:** A Working Guide for Adult Children of Alcoholics and Other Dysfunctional Families. Recovery Publications, San Diego, 1987.

Fuhlrodt RL: **Psychodrama:** Its Applications to ACoA and Substance Abuse Treatment. Perrin & Treggett, Rutherford, NJ, 800-321-7912, 1989.

Goodman J: Laughing Matters quoted in Friedman M: A laugh a day. *New Realities.* Jan.-Feb., p. 39-42, 1988.

Gravitz HL, Bowden JD: **Recovery:** A Guide for Adult Children of Alcoholics. Simon & Schuster, New York, 1985. One of the most practical books for ACoAs.

Greenleaf J: Surviving The Visit Home: Coping with Your Family of Origin at Holiday Time. Greenleaf, Los Angeles, 1987 (audiotape and pamphlet).

Grof S: **The Adventure of Self-Discovery.** Dimensions of Consciousness and New Perspectives in Psychotherapy and Inner Exploration. State Univ NY Press, Albany, 1988. This book is about *breathwork* in the form of holonomic integration or holotropic therapy. See p. 154 for brief description.

Hay L: Talk on Healing Techniques. Phoenix, 1987.

Helmstetter S: **What To Say When You Talk To Yourself.** William Morrow, New York, 1985.

Hendricks G: **Learning To Love Yourself:** A Guide To Becoming Centered. Prentice-Hall, New York, 1982. A practical guide to the topic. Gentle and powerful.

Hendrix H: **Getting The Love You Want:** A Guide for Couples. Henry Holt, New York, 1988. Useful for AC couples.

Jacoby M: **The Analytic Encounter:** Transference and Human Relationships. Inner City Books, Toronto, 1984. A basic book on transference from a Freudian and Jungian perspective.

James JW: **The Grief Recovery Handbook,** Harper & Row, San Francisco, 1988.

Johnson RA: **Inner Work:** Using Dreams and Active Imagination for Personal Growth. Harper & Row, San Francisco, 1986.

Johnson R: **Active Imagination** (two audiotapes), Credence Cassettes, Box 414291, Kansas City, MO. Two talks on audiotape that summarize what is in the above cited book, **Inner Work**, by an experienced Jungian therapist.

Jones A: **Creative Thought Remedies.** DeVorss & Co, Marina del Rey, CA, 1986. A psycho-spiritual approach to values, feelings and relationships. Many useful affirmations.

Jourard SM: **The Transparent Self.** Van Nostrand, New York, 1971.

Lazaris: Series of Spiritual-Psychological Teachings. Concept Synergy, 302 S. County Rd, Ste 109, Palm Beach, FL 33408. Teachings on videotape, audiotape, books and workshops on spiritual psychology. I use Lazaris' teachings in my descriptions of how our beliefs, thoughts, etc. influence our life (Chapter 25).

Lee J: **The Flying Boy:** Healing The Wounded Man. Health Communications, Deerfield Beach, 1989. A personal story of an adult child in recovery. Describes the emotional pain, awareness, responsibility and work that it took for the author to heal.

McGoldrick M, Gerson R: **Genograms in Family Assessment.** WW Norton, NY, 1985. More detailed approaches to using the "family tree" or genogram, using families of famous people as some illustrations.

Miller EE, Sheaver DR: **Blossoming:** Growing Beyond the Limits of Your Family. Source, Box W, Stanford, CA 94305, 415-328-1717. 1985. Healing guided imagery on audiotapes for adult children.

National Association for Children of Alcoholics, 31706 Coast Highway, Ste 201, South Laguna, CA 92677, 714-499-3889.

O'Toole D: Arvie Aardvark and other writings, personal communication, Baltimore, 1989.

O'Toole, D: **Healing & Growing Through Grief.** Rainbow Connection, 477 Hannah Branch Rd., Burnsville, NC 28714. 1988.

Palmer H: **Creativism.** Stars Edge, 900 Markham Woods Rd, Longwood, FL, 1987.

Pennebaker J: SMU study, Dallas, 1986.

Progoff I: **The Practice of Process Meditation.** Dialogue House Library, New York, 1980.

Rodegast P, Stanton J: **Emmanuel's Book:** A Manual for Living Comfortably in the Cosmos. Bantam, New York, 1985. One of the best introductions to spirituality for adult children.

Rodegast P, Stanton J: **Emmanuel's Book II,** The Choice for Love. Bantam, New York, 1989. A continuation of Emmanuel's wise and beautiful psychospiritual teachings. Better than the first.

Simos BG: **A Time to Grieve:** Loss as a Universal Human Experience. Family Services Association of America, New York, 1979. Detailed summary of the entire grieving process. One of the best.

Sisson CP: **Rebirthing Made Easy.** Hay House, Santa Monica, CA, 1987. An introduction to rebirthing.

Stone H, Winkelman S: **Embracing Ourselves: The Voice Dialogue Manual.** New World Library, San Rafael, CA, 1988.

Stone H, Winkelman S: **Embracing Each Other: Relationship as Teacher, Healer and Guide.** New World Library, San Rafael, CA, 1989.
In their map of the psyche, what they call the "vulnerable child" is in my map a combination of the feeling child, compassionate child, and unconditionally loving child (see pages viii and 28 of this book and page 130 of *HCW*). And what they call the "aware ego" is what bridges the experiencing, struggling and growing child and the intuitive and creative child in my map. Remember that "the map is not the territory" *and* that maps are useful.

Storr A: **Solitude:** A Return to the Self. Free Press, New York, 1988. Excellent book on nourishing and growing time alone.

Travis JW, Ryan RS: **Wellness Workbook** (2nd ed), Ten Speed Press, Box 7123, Berkeley, CA, 1988.

Vaughan F: **Awakening Intuition.** Anchor/Doubleday, New York, 1987. An authoritative and practical discussion of intuition with some ideas on how to differentiate it from impulsiveness.

Wegscheider-Cruse S: **Choicemaking:** For Co-dependents, Adult Children and Spirituality Seekers. Health Communications, Pompano Beach, FL, 1985.

Wells JS: **A Psychology of Love:** A Perspective Of Balance In An Unbalanced World. Pvt. printing. Rt 3, Box 456, Hillsborough, NC 27278, 1988. A book of sayings, principles and practical concepts about possibly our most misunderstood four-letter word.

Whitfield CL: "Children of Alcoholics: Treatment Issues." In *Services for Children of Alcoholics,* NIAAA Research Monograph 4, 1979.

Whitfield CL: **Core Issues in Recovery for Adult Children, Co-dependents and Chemical Dependents,** vols. 1, 2 and 3. ACCESS, P.O. Box 30380, Indianapolis, IN 46230, 800-234-8280, 1988, '89 & '90. Audiotapes of workshops on core issues and basic dynamics in recovery. Much of this material will be described in a new book in process called **Wisdom To Know The Difference** (see below).

Whitfield CL: **Healing The Child Within,** Health Communications, Deerfield Beach, FL, 1987. Book and audiotape from your local bookstore or 800-851-9100.

Whitfield CL: **Healing The Child Within** and **Spirituality For Adult Children, Co-dependents And Chemical Dependents** (two separate audiotape sets). ACCESS, P.O. Box 30380, Indianapolis, IN 46230, 1988. Workshops on audiotape.

Whitfield CL: **Healing The Child Within.** Audiotape of one-day workshop, Listen to Learn Taping Services, San Diego, 800-537-8273, 1988. Similar workshop audiotape set available from ARC Taping Services, New York, 1989.

Whitfield CL: **Spirituality In Recovery** (also called **Alcoholism, Attachments And Spirituality**). Pre-print available from Perrin & Treggett, Rutherford, NJ, 800-321-7912, 1985.

Whitfield CL: **Spirituality In Recovery:** What it is and how to use it, parts 1 and 2 (audiotape set). Listen to Learn Taping Services, San Diego, 800-537-8273. Weekend workshop, Aug 1988. A two-day workshop describing some fundamentals of spirituality in recovery. Lecture and discussion is supplemented by two guided imageries, soundtrack from A Meeting With Emmanuel videotape and people telling their stories of recovery and spirituality.

Whitfield CL: **Boundaries And Limits** in Relationships and Recovery. Health Communications, Deerfield Beach, FL (manuscript in process for 1991).

Whitfield CL: **Toward A New Paradigm In The Helping Professions.** ACCESS, P.O. Box 30380, Indianapolis, IN 46230, 800-234-8280 Mar 1989. A one-hour audiotape talk on how the Adult Child and Recovery movements are beginning to change the world view, practice and personal life of many helping professionals and its potential in the helping professions.

Whitfield CL: **The Transpersonal Psychology Of Jesus Christ.** Listen to Learn Taping Service, San Diego, 800-537-8273. Oct 1988. A one hour and 15-minute audiotape introduction on the expanded and ongoing psycho-spiritual teachings of the Christ. Begins to differentiate what Christ really taught and teaches from what others say he taught.

Whitfield CL: **Wisdom To Know The Difference:** Transforming Co-dependence Into Healthy Relationships. New book in process, estimated completion around 1991 or 1992. This book will complete a trilogy, with **Healing The Child Within/A Gift To Myself** and **Spirituality In Recovery,** wherein we can examine our relationship with our self, others and our Higher Power. My book on boundaries will supplement these.

Other Books By . . .
Health Communications

ADULT CHILDREN OF ALCOHOLICS
Janet Woititz
Over a year on *The New York Times* Best-Seller list, this book is the primer on Adult Children of Alcoholics.
ISBN 0-932194-15-X $6.95

STRUGGLE FOR INTIMACY
Janet Woititz
Another best-seller, this book gives insightful advice on learning to love more fully.
ISBN 0-932194-25-7 $6.95

DAILY AFFIRMATIONS: For Adult Children of Alcoholics
Rokelle Lerner
These positive affirmations for every day of the year paint a mental picture of your life as you choose it to be.
ISBN 0-932194-27-3 $6.95

CHOICEMAKING: For Co-dependents, Adult Children and Spirituality Seekers — Sharon Wegscheider-Cruse
This useful book defines the problems and solves them in a positive way.
ISBN 0-932194-26-5 $9.95

LEARNING TO LOVE YOURSELF: Finding Your Self-Worth
Sharon Wegscheider-Cruse
"Self-worth is a choice, not a birthright," says the author as she shows us how we can choose positive self-esteem.
ISBN 0-932194-39-7 $7.95

BRADSHAW ON: THE FAMILY: A Revolutionary Way of Self-Discovery
John Bradshaw
The host of the nationally televised series of the same name shows us how families can be healed and individuals can realize full potential.
ISBN 0-932194-54-0 $9.95

HEALING THE CHILD WITHIN:
Discovery and Recovery for Adult Children of Dysfunctional Families
Charles Whitfield
Dr. Whitfield defines, describes and discovers how we can reach our Child Within to heal and nurture our woundedness.
ISBN 0-932194-40-0 $8.95

Enterprise Center, 3201 S.W. 15th Street,
Deerfield Beach, FL 33442
1-800-851-9100

Health Communications, Inc.

Daily Affirmation Books from . . .
Health Communications

GENTLE REMINDERS FOR CO-DEPENDENTS: *Daily Affirmations*
Mitzi Chandler
With insight and humor, Mitzi Chandler takes the co-dependent and the adult child through the year. Gentle Reminders is for those in recovery who seek to enjoy the miracle each day brings.
ISBN 1-55874-020-1 $6.95

TIME FOR JOY: *Daily Affirmations*
Ruth Fishel
With quotations, thoughts and healing energizing affirmations these daily messages address the fears and imperfections of being human, guiding us through self-acceptance to a tangible peace and the place within where there is *time for joy.*
ISBN 0-932194-82-6 $6.95

CRY HOPE: *Positive Affirmations For Healthy Living*
Jan Veltman
This book gives positive daily affirmations for seekers and those in recovery. Every day is a new adventure, and change is a challenge.
ISBN 0-932194-74-5 $6.95

SAY YES TO LIFE: *Daily Affirmations For Recovery*
Father Leo Booth
These meditations take you through the year day by day with Father Leo Booth, looking for answers and sometimes discovering that there are none. Father Leo tells us, "For the recovering compulsive person God is too important to miss — may you find Him now."
IBN 0-932194-46-X $6.95

DAILY AFFIRMATIONS: *For Adult Children of Alcoholics*
Rokelle Lerner
Affirmations are a way to discover personal awareness, growth and spiritual potential, and self-regard. Reading this book gives us an opportunity to nurture ourselves, learn who we are and what we want to become.
ISBN 0-932194-47-3
(Little Red Book) $6.95
(New Cover Edition) $6.95

Enterprise Center, 3201 S.W. 15th Street,
Deerfield Beach, FL 33442
1-800-851-9100

 **Health Communications, Inc.**